Radical
Manifestation

The Fine Art of Creating
the Life You Want . . .

*Using Spiritual Intelligence to manifest money,
weight loss, happiness
and more*

COLIN C. TIPPING

Copyright © 2006, Colin C.Tipping.

"RADICAL Manifestation,
The Fine Art of Creating the Life You Want"

Published in April, 2006

Printed in the United States of America

RADICAL Forgiveness, Radical Empowerment and Radical Manifestation are Trademarks of Global 13 Publications, Inc.

ISBN 0-9704814-9-7

Global 13 Publications, Inc.
26 Briar Gate Lane,
Marietta GA 30066

Website: www.radicalempowerment.com

Cover Design: Tiger Rock

Proof Reading: Dana Dobson

Dedicated to my wife,
JoAnn,
who unstintingly empowers me
with her love.

Contents

LIST OF ILLUSTRATIONS

Introduction

Something interesting is happening. Suddenly there is an upsurge of interest in, and an increasing awareness of, the possibility that life is not just something that happens to us, but that we actually have a hand in creating it through our consciousness. Web sites abound with programs for increasing our capacity to manifest what we want in our lives. PBS has run extended programs on *"The Power of Intention"* with Dr. Wayne Dyer, and even more recently on the subject of *"Inspiration."* Will Marré is another featured author on PBS who speaks about *"Creating Your Dream Life."* Robert Kiyosaki has recently presented his *"Rich Dad—Poor Dad"* seminar about prosperity on PBS. Bookstores are featuring a great many books on creative manifestation, prosperity and wealth, including *"Ask and it is Given,"* by Abraham-Hicks.

Underlying all of these approaches is the idea that if we understand and use the Law of Attraction, we can create the reality we want. There is every reason to believe that this is so, and that the power to manifest our reality is inherent in every one of us.

This used to be a matter of pure faith and was routinely dismissed by mainstream thinking as "New-Age babble." Since quantum physics and other scientific disciplines have given it credibility and generally support the notion, at least in theory, this has now given way to an attitude of careful consideration.

The skepticism arises not only in those who prefer not to believe in the idea that we create our own reality through our thoughts and beliefs, but also in those of us who desperately want to believe it. That's because we are struggling to make things happen in our own lives and are failing to do so. Not surprisingly, our skepticism arises out of frustration and a sense of failure. The reason for our difficulty is two-fold.

Firstly, our vibration is probably not high enough to empower us in the conscious use of the Law of Attraction so that we get what we consciously want. Rather, we actually attract to ourselves what our subconscious minds want. This is invariably at odds with our conscious desires.

[**Note:** This is not the same thing as when your soul gives you what your soul needs for the purpose of healing and growing. That is high vibration activity that is Spirit-led, not Ego-led.]

Put another way, we are prevented from having what we want because our subconscious minds block it with low vibration energy that exists as core negative beliefs, fear, guilt, anger, resentment and other forms of negative energy.

Secondly, we have not yet made the shift in consciousness at a deep enough level to be able to trust that if we surrender everything to Spirit we will get what we need. Willingness to surrender is a key part of the manifestation process.

We devour the wise words in the books we read, we repeat affirmations and we nod adoringly in agreement when we listen to Wayne Dyer and Deepak Chopra. We do the meditations, consult the stars, Fung Shui our homes and offices and yet, in spite of it all, we go on as usual in our daily lives, trying to make things happen through force, planning, control, work and struggle. Not surprisingly then, we do not seem to manifest what we want.

We do indeed live in exciting times, but the problem is that we need to realize that we are between paradigms. We still live in the old one, with its belief in shortage and limitation, but we are trying to work with the new one which rests upon the revolutionary idea that there is no shortage of anything, that the Universe is a place of infinite abundance and that we have the power to draw from the field of infinite possibility anything we want.

We must have compassion for ourselves and recognize that we need tools to help us to straddle the two paradigms. We need tools that recognize and accept our lack of belief and certitude about the new reality, while at the same time allowing us to practice the art of creative manifestation and to consistently experience success with it. Without some sort of technology to assist us in this, we are doomed to failure. Words alone on a page or on a CD are not enough. We are still too invested in the old paradigm.

Such tools for *Radical Manifestation* are already available and well-proven because they are based on the same powerful technology behind *Radical Forgiveness,* which has helped thousands of people over the last ten years or so. I have always believed that spiritual growth only comes about through some kind of practice or through the use of tools that take us into the experience of transformation at the energetic level, rather than at the intellectual level. The tools need to engage us physically, emotionally and spiritually.

The tools of *Radical Forgiveness,* and now those of *Radical Empowerment* and *Radical Manifestation* look like mere worksheets, CDs and DVDs, but they are really energy instruments that connect us to our spiritual intelligence. That is the part of us that knows how to connect with the "unified field of consciousness and field of infinite possibility." Once that happens, and we get our minds out of the way, then manifestation can occur.

Having described one of the things that makes this approach unique, let me now return to the other factor that makes it even more so. It is that my decade of working with and developing the tools of *Radical Forgiveness* is paying off to the extent that it provides us with a proven way of raising our vibration to the level at which we become automatically empowered manifestors of our own reality.

I mentioned earlier that what keeps our vibration low and blocks our empowerment is our commitment to blaming others, holding onto our resentment, fear, guilt, shame and anger, and generally being a victim. *Radical Forgiveness* enables people to release all that negativity in a very short space of time. That has the effect of bringing one's energy back into present time and raising our vibration.

The combination of *Radical Forgiveness* (to heal the past and give you a way to deal with the present), and *Radical Empowerment* (to create the future), is a powerful one. It is powerful because it is a practical, down-to-earth and simple way to manifest everything you want.

[**Author's Note:** If you are reading this book as a constituent part of the multi-media program entitled, *"Colin Tipping's Radical Empowerment Program,"* you will already have all the *Radical Forgiveness* and *Radical Manifestion* tools and resources available to you in the form of CDs, DVDs, book, on-line programs and worksheets.]

5

If you are reading this book as a stand-alone item and are not familiar with the *Radical Forgiveness* technology, you might find it quite helpful to take a look at the web site, *www.radicalforgiveness.com*. There are some free, downloadable tools and a free on-line *Radical Forgiveness Worksheet Tutorial* available on there for your use.

For information about *"Colin Tipping's Radical Empowerment Program,"* refer to the Appendix, Page 193.

PART ONE

The Transformation
of Consciousness

RADICAL MANIFESTATION

Chapter 1
Empowerment as Transformation

E mpowerment is commonly equated with becoming more powerful in ways that align with becoming more efficient, more educated, better trained, more assertive, more competitive, more motivated, more skilled, more focused, working smarter, leveraging time, money and resources more wisely and so on. These are all good things to do and to become in order to be more powerful in the material sense and to be more "successful" in the external world.

R*adical Empowerment* is not about those things at all. It is about an inner transformation. It involves turning your whole way of looking at the world completely upside down, overturning all your belief systems, values and assumptions. *Radical Empowerment* occurs at the deepest levels of your being and brings you to the point where you are able to manifest anything you want. **The outcome of *Radical Empowerment*, therefore, is *Radical Manifestation*.**

9

Empowerment at this level of transformation lies in embracing a wholly different paradigm of reality, a world view that enables you to claim your true power as a spiritual being having a spiritual experience in a human world and a physical body.

Once this happens you begin to operate at that higher level of functioning where you are not just the effect in a cause and effect world, but always the cause. It is about realizing that you live in a totally abundant universe that enables you to consciously create your world as you want it to be and where there is no separation, and where love is all there is.

Radical Empowerment is about being totally willing to let go and align vibrationally with the Source of All Being which lies within each one of us and from which we draw our true power and our ability to manifest reality. *Radical Manifestation* is about using our inborn spiritual intelligence — that part of our mind that is always in touch with what our soul needs and can bring forth. Our spiritual intelligence operates at a higher level of functioning than mental or emotional intelligence. It knows how to connect with Universal Intelligence and to be in the flow of abundance that is the natural state of the Universe.

Willingness
Notice that, in the first line of the paragraph above, I said it was about being 'willing' to let go and align with Source. The only requirement is that we be ***willing*** to raise our level of functioning and live from the new paradigm, not

to be 100 percent there. Be w*illing* to trust and surrender; be *willing* to drop our attachment; be *willing* to forgive and so on, and to love ourselves when we fall short.

The Key to Our Spiritual Evolution

Willingness is the key to becoming radically empowered because, even though certain events, experiences, epiphanies etc., may kick-start one's transformation, or accelerate it at certain points along the way, it is rarely an instantaneous experience. True transformation is an evolutionary phenomenon. It involves our making constant adjustments in our values, beliefs, assumptions and behaviors based on the feedback that comes both from the external world and from within.

It's our willingness to perceive and respond to that feedback that determines how quickly and how easily we transform. It's our willingness to drop our need to be right that will allow us to keep making those evolutionary jumps in our awareness and our ways of thinking and being. It's only our resistance to letting go of our existing beliefs, assumptions and behaviors that slows us down and makes it a struggle.

Let It Be Easy

Assuming that you have a profound commitment to your self-development and spiritual growth, this book and the multi-media program associated with it* is designed to make the transformation easier. It gives you tools that will

---

* See Appendix I and www.radicalempowerment.com

11

ease you through it, reduce the fear, minimize the resistance and pre-empt the struggle. Rest assured, *Radical Manifestation* CAN be easy once you become willing to accept the new paradigm. You will be surprised how all the things connected with the current paradigm (money, success, relationships, career, goals, etc.) will fall into place automatically.

Chapter 2
Manifesting Scarcity

Our existing world view that almost everyone subscribes to at this time does not work for *Radical Manifestation.* The prevailing beliefs, assumptions and values simply don't support it.

The current paradigm supports the fundamental assumption that shortage is inevitable and a self-evident fact of life. As a result of vesting a lot of power in the belief in scarcity, we have actually created that reality in numerous, and in some cases, horrific forms. The vast majority of the people on this planet suffer from grinding poverty, which is how the belief in shortage is expressed as reality in most parts of the world.

At the opposite end of the scale, scarcity is purposefully created in order to increase value. For example, diamonds are extremely expensive, not because they are scarce but because they are purposefully withheld from the market in order to give the illusion of shortage and rarity. Scarcity and value are inextricably linked and shortage is created in order to increase perceived value. Our whole economic system is based on the notion of shortage. Don't look for poverty to be eradicated soon. It is too profitable.

Shortage at all Levels

Even if we are not amongst the very poorest of people, who doesn't find themselves coping with shortage in one way or another and see it as one of their greatest challenges? Even the very rich crave more and have a terrible fear of losing what they have.

Our logical mind will always come up with all sorts of arguments to defend our position that shortage is real. It is, after all, our everyday experience and is the main justification for most of what we do with our lives. We are not likely to give up that idea easily.

In fact, I would expect that you are probably still linking the whole idea of *Radical Manifestation* to the idea of having more of what you see as scarce. Why wouldn't you? It seems self-evident. But it is only that way because we have created it according to our beliefs.

Our ability to manifest easily is effectively turned off and blocked by those beliefs. That means then, that in order to really transform and become radically empowered, we need to undergo a profound paradigm shift. So what is a paradigm shift? And to what set of assumptions, beliefs, concepts, values and behaviors are we shifting that would support our transformation?

Chapter 3
Paradigm Shift

A paradigm shift is certainly not anything minor. It is a major restructuring of one's total cognitive map relative to a major field of knowledge, understanding and practice, and it can take a long time to achieve.

By virtue of the fact that you are reading this book and have read others that tend to be more aligned with the new paradigm we are about to discuss, you are probably already in the process of shifting, and have been so doing for some years. However, you can dramatically accelerate that transformation by following the advice in this book and using the tools it refers to throughout and describes in the Appendix.

Medical Paradigms Shifting
To illustrate the nature of a paradigm shift, it might be helpful to look at an example of one with which most

people are familiar and may even have had some experience. I refer to how the world of medicine is shifting uneasily from the existing paradigm of western allopathic medicine to a new one based on energy medicine.

For the last 400 years, modern allopathic medicine has held sway as the predominant form of medicine in the Western world. The vast majority of people accept, even now, all the major premises on which it was based and believe it to be self-evidently the "right" way to practice medicine.

In the last 20 years, however, this paradigm has been challenged and there has been a perceptible shift towards energy medicine. It has been mostly a consumer-driven shift with the medical profession fighting it every inch of the way. However, since people are now spending so much of their money on various forms of energy medicine such as acupuncture, homeopathy, herbalism, chiropractic and so on, the medical doctors are now having to take notice.

Traditional medicine and energy medicine are based on fundamentally different premises. Traditional, allopathic medicine is rooted in the world of physical science and is largely about intervening with drugs and/or surgery. Energy medicine works with subtle bodies that allopathic medicine simply does not recognize and, rather than intervening, focuses on stimulating the body to heal itself.

It is true that energy medicine and allopathic medicine can possibly coexist side-by-side in an uneasy relationship, but they can never come together in any coherent fashion and at the same time maintain their integrity.

How a Paradigm Shift Occurs
Sociologist Thomas Kuhn described three stages in the birth of a new paradigm.

Stage 1. There is total resistance to it and ridicule of those proposing it.

Stage 2. There is an attempt to explain it by referencing it back to the previous paradigm using the old language and concepts.

Stage 3. Acceptance of its being completely self-evident.

If you are even vaguely familiar with how things stand with both these forms of medicine, you will probably recognize that we are only just beginning to emerge from Kuhn's first stage. And that's only because the public have voted with their pocketbooks and have switched in large numbers to alternative energy medicine (acupuncture, homeopathy, chiropractic, Reiki, Healing Touch and the like).

Losing the Essence
This has forced the medical establishment to begin talking about energy medicine but, as yet, only in the language of traditional allopathic medicine. As you would expect, they completely fail to convey the essence of energy medicine.

A good example of this is where doctors refer to meditation as a "relaxation technique." They just don't get it that one meditates, not to relax, but in order to focus the mind to become receptive to the still, small voice within that connects us the Source of our being. That the body relaxes during meditation is helpful, but it is certainly not the purpose of the exercise.

17

Media Lag

You only have to watch "20/20," "Dateline," or "60 Minutes" to realize that ridicule of the proponents of energy medicine is still the underlying attitude in the media and, by and large, within the medical profession itself. The justification is that it (energy medicine) is scientifically "unproven" and therefore not valid. No one mentions the fact that at least 40 percent of standard medical practice has never been scientifically validated. The figure is probably higher. There are many things that are simply not appropriate for double-blind trials, surgical procedures being one of them. The test in those cases is whether or not they seem to work, which is precisely the test applied to energy medicine. Funny how it is okay for the former and not the latter. In the case of both acupuncture and homeopathy, they have been found to work well for 5,000 and 7,000 years respectively.

They also cite safety concerns; that energy medicine is not tested and proven safe by the Food and Drug Administration. But seldom do they ever mention that by the British Medical Association's own admission, over 150,000 people die each year because of doctor errors. The figure is probably much higher, but what is interesting is that even at 150,000, no one is outraged. If one person were to die through acupuncture, it would be front-page news and there would be moves in Congress to have it banned.

Positionality

What becomes obvious is that none of this has anything to do with logic or even common sense. It's not about the facts or even science. It's simply a question of whether your consciousness is at stage one, two or three. It's a matter of where you stand, or what position you take in defence of the model that you have in your head about, in this case, medicine in general. These are the things that determine the nature of the debate, not science, logic or training. In actual fact, it appears that in the case of energy medicine, the public is way ahead of the media and the medical profession. They have tried it; it seems to work, so they go back for more. It's that simple.

Investment in the Old Paradigm
The public is not much invested in either paradigm, except to the extent that they find them efficacious to their health. That's their only interest. Doctors, on the other hand, have many years of education, training and money invested in the allopathic approach, so naturally they will be the last to accept the new paradigm. It's the same with all forms of "conventional wisdom." Look what happened to Galileo when he challenged the idea that the Earth was the center of the Universe!

In the next two chapters we'll look at where we are in the process of making the paradigm shift, from the old paradigm of how life works based on Newtonian physics, Darwinism, duality, separation and limitation, etc., to the new paradigm based on Quantum Physics — the unified field, oneness and infinite abundance. What we are likely to find is that we are in about the same stage with this one as we are with the medical paradigm shift described above. Perhaps they are different aspects of the same thing.

19

Chapter 4
Descartes and Darwin

Everyone has in their own mind a highly developed model of the world and their place in that world. We even call it our "world view." Another name for it is our cosmology. It is not necessarily uniform from culture to culture, and in some cases it is radically different. To the extent that everyone in a particular culture shares a relatively stable world view, it becomes the agreed paradigm about how the world works and how life itself operates. To those who share that world view, it seems nothing less than self-evidently true — until, that is, it begins to shift.

So let's first examine the paradigm that has determined values, beliefs, assumptions and behaviors in the Western world for the last 400 years, and then look at the features of the emergent one that will provide us with the power to emerge as self-actualized spiritual beings having spiritual experiences in human form.

Rene Descartes (1596 - 1650)

It has been the role of philosophers down the ages to figure out the meaning of life and how it all works. The French philosopher and scientist Rene Descartes is the one largely responsible for the scientific/rational paradigm that we have now. He is the one famously credited with the dictum "I think, therefore I am." He was convinced that science and mathematics could and should be used to explain everything in nature. The human body was to be understood as a complex machine that could be simply reduced to its constituent parts — molecules, atoms, and other measurables.

This led to a very mechanistic and reductionist view of reality. Anything that could not be measured or objectively quantified was denied as unworthy of consideration because it was always in doubt. Mind and body were considered to be quite separate.

Sir Isaac Newton (1642 - 1727)

Newtonian physics gave support to this mechanistic viewpoint in the way it described how the physical world worked in terms of cause and effect and so on. Newton's views held sway until the early part of the 20th century, when the quantum physicists overturned his theories in favor of quantum mechanical theory. However, Newtonian physics are still applicable to everyday life and are still relevant today, except insofar as we now realize that they are not the whole story by any means.

Charles Darwin (1809 - 1882)

The other person who had an enormous influence in the formation of our current paradigm was Charles Darwin. His Theory of Evolution held that everything has evolved by a process of random chance and by selective mutations based on the mechanism of natural selection and the survival of the fittest.

Life is Luck

This revolutionary idea, combined with the new mechanistic and reductionist viewpoint of Descartes and Newton, became the model for how we should view our own life — as being nothing more than a string of unrelated, random events. They happen for no particular reason other than chance or the direct consequences of our own actions or those of people around us. Life simply happens. There is little or no meaning in it and very little purpose other than to survive. You do the best you can with what you've got, procreate in order to continue the lineage, and then die at a the appropriate time. The focus is on the external world, especially on our own physical body, its comfort and the satisfaction of desires.

Cause and Effect

Under this prevailing paradigm, our belief is that the objective world out there exists separately from us, and our consciousness is inconsequential to it. It is a cause and effect world and we are the effect — never the cause. Our awareness is largely a matter of billions of neurons firing in our brain every millisecond, and our bodies are simply elegant machines composed of atoms, molecules and

23

chemicals. It's all pretty impersonal, indifferent and meaningless. "Life's a bitch, and then you die," as they say.

Sharks

Darwin's theory and his notion of the survival of the fittest creates the "shark" environment, or "dog-eat-dog" philosophy that legitimizes competitive, discriminatory and even cruel, dispassionate behavior towards other people. It is actually called Social Darwinism, and as such is accorded validity.

Fear-Based System

What arises from this cause and effect view of life is the idea that if we are not to be buffeted around by the meaningless vagaries of life, we must do as much as possible to gain control over it. Otherwise we will not survive. That's what makes it a fear-based system. If life itself is uncaring, dispassionate and neutral, that means we are totally on our own. So we plan, organize, educate ourselves, build physical structures, produce products and do our very best to control every aspect of our lives and everything around us, primarily with the aim of achieving a high level of physical comfort and security. And then, for everything that we cannot control, we buy a lot of insurance and hope that nothing unexpected happens. When it does, we are devastated and feel totally victimized by life.

In short, the current paradigm is based on a profound belief in separation and duality driven by fear, judgment, blame and guilt, the result of which is continual conflict. Even God is seen as the judging father "up-there" who is bent on punishing us for separating from Him and for not being good.

Chapter 5
Metaphysical Reality

The new paradigm towards which we are moving holds a metaphysical viewpoint, and it could hardly be more different to the one we are moving away from. The basic spiritual assumptions and beliefs inherent in this paradigm are as follows.

Oneness and Interconnectivity

Whereas the current paradigm emphasizes individual separateness, differences, inequality and hierarchical models that put man above everything else and accord him dominion over the natural order, the metaphysical paradigm emphasizes the exact opposite. The fundamental idea is that oneness is the underlying principle of existence and that Love is the basic unifying force in the Universe.

Even though there are differences between things, renowned physicist, David Bohm, says that everything in the Universe is part of a single continuum and that our tendency to fragment the world into parts and ignore the dynamic interconnectedness of all things accounts for most of our problems. Life is a wholistic experience. When we realize that we are all one, that has enormous implications for how we look at everything, including values like justice, equality, freedom and responsibility, and how we view our own relationship to the animal kingdom and the planet itself.

Only Love is Real

There is only one energy in the Universe, and it is Love. When we feel emotions like anger, guilt, fear and sadness, the feeling is actually love distorted by the beliefs attached to the feeling. Every action is either an expression of love or a call for love.

The Universe is Perfection in Action

The Universe is an expression of perfection in that everything works exactly as it should and everything is totally purposeful in supporting the whole — even when it appears not to be so.

Everything Happens for a Reason

This is an extension of the idea of perfection and is the basic principle of *Radical Forgiveness*. Things don't happen TO you; they happen FOR you. Your soul creates these situations as opportunities for you to learn and grow.

The Divine Plan

Whereas meaning beyond mere existence is absent in the paradigm of objective reality, the metaphysical paradigm sees everything in life as being chock full of meaning, even if it is way beyond our ability to fathom what it might be. It recognizes that everything that happens is purposeful and part of the Divine plan, even if we have no idea what the purpose might be, what the plan is, or whose plan it might be.

Contrary to the popular view, therefore, life is not a random set of events without purpose or intelligence. What appears to be haphazard is really the unfoldment of a Divine plan that is totally purposeful in terms of our spiritual evolution. It is a dynamic plan that changes every time we make a decision, but it is always in a state of divine perfection.

The Bigger Picture
Whereas the existing paradigm requires physical proof and measurement of existence, the new paradigm asks us to trust our inner knowing that there is more to reality than that which we can register with our five senses or known instruments. We have to surrender to the idea that reality is far bigger than we have the capacity to comprehend. *(Maybe one day we will be able to see the big picture and all will be revealed, but at this time it remains obscured.)*

The Universe Handles the Details
Not being privy to the big picture, we simply don't know all the possible variables of a situation that confront us. Infinite Intelligence does, and knows also what is in our best interests. When we surrender a problem to Infinite Intelligence, we discover how easy events tend to unfold and how easy it is to manifest the world we want.

Spiritual Beings Having a Human Experience

Even though "spiritual amnesia" is necessary for the experiment to work, our soul has made a choice to incarnate in order to be totally immersed in a finite world of separation, duality, change and suffering. This is to enable our soul to evolve into the experience of being Love. To achieve that, we have to transcend everything that appears to be unlike Love. The human experience provides precisely that challenge. The old paradigm actually serves us quite well for this purpose and is perfect in that sense. We also do it to contribute to the expansion of the mind of Universal Intelligence (God).

Spiritual Beings Having a Spiritual Experience In a Human Body

Once we have awakened at the right, predetermined point in our lives and have become more aware of the truth of who we are, we begin to move into an awareness of this alternative paradigm. We then realize that we are spiritual beings but at the same time continue to be fully grounded in the human experience — mainly to be of service to others.

We Have Free Will

Even though we have incarnated with the blessing of the All That Is, Infinite Intelligence, God or whatever name you want to give to it, it is our choice as to how we create our experience, what lessons we choose and how we create them. We have complete free will to do it however we want to, and to find our own way home.

Spiritual Intelligence

Since our spiritual intelligence will always move us in the direction of healing, it will keep on creating situations that offer us the opportunity to see the limitations in our thinking or unconscious beliefs. It attracts people into our lives to mirror those beliefs, or lovingly "act out" the parts repeatedly until we heal the misperception and awaken to the truth of who we are.

Enemies as Teachers and Healing Angels

The people we dislike the most are our greatest teachers, for they may be offering us the opportunity to heal by either:

(a) mirroring what we hate in ourselves and have denied, repressed and projected onto them.

(b) forcing us to look at something we have repressed and which remains a core belief or unhealed trauma.

(c) keeping us on track with our mission.

Life Is A Mirror

What appears to be happening in the objective world is merely illusion — it is just a projection of our consciousness (our unconscious beliefs, ideas, attitudes, etc.). To know what these are, look what is showing up in your life. Life is simply a mirror and it will show you what your beliefs are. For example, if you believe that you can't trust people, you will continually attract people into your life who will betray you. We are very committed to being right about our beliefs so we unconsciously create all sorts of ways to prove or validate them. That's how powerful we are, and we don't know it!

Nothing to Forgive

Whereas the focus in the old paradigm was on judgment, anger, blame and punishment, the new paradigm holds that since everything happens for a reason, there is no such thing as right or wrong. It just is. From the spiritual perspective, therefore, nothing wrong or right is ever happening and there is nothing to forgive. Forgiveness is moot.

"Out There" versus "In Here"

Whereas in the old paradigm, the focus was always on the objective world out there, the new paradigm recognizes that the world "out there" is a projection of the world "in here," and that there is no separation between them. It is all one. Even God now lives within each one of us instead of "up there." We are now one with God and God is Love — the unifying force in the Universe.

Spiritual Energy

Whereas the old paradigm existed within the constraints of three-dimensional reality, with religion as something separate, the new paradigm puts spirituality (not religion) front and center and expands our notions of reality to include dimensions beyond form and space that are spiritual in nature. String theory is close to proving that everything in the Universe is composed of tiny strings or loops of energy and that what they eventually manifest as in the physical world is a function of their vibrational frequency.

Energy Bodies

Instead of regarding our bodies as machines, we now see them as a set of interrelating energy fields and that health is a matter of balancing energy. In my work with corporations,** I have them see their own corporation not as an amalgam of departments, buildings, systems and so on, but a complex energy field composed of all the energy fields of the people who work there.

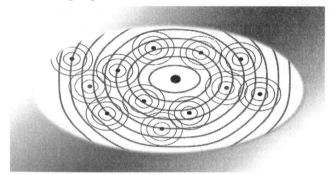

Fig:1 The Energy Field of a Corporation

They are now beginning to understand that corporate health depends on the health of the corporate energy field, and that, in turn, depends on everyone in the corporation having energy fields that are clear and healthy.

Cause or Effect
Whereas the old paradigm places us totally at the mercy of life with no part to play in the creation of it, the new paradigm offers us the opportunity to be not just the effect in a cause and effect world, but the cause. This is not just talk. The physicists have proven that consciousness is the creative force in the Universe and that matter manifests as a consequence of our observation of it.

**The Quantum Energy Management System is the corporate version of Radical Forgiveness. See Appendix, Page 200.

31

Matter can exist as both a wave and a particle. Prior to its manifesting, it exists as a wave form — a potential. It manifests when it converts from being a wave to being a particle. What determines whether it is a wave or a particle is our consciousness. So, far from being inconsequential to creation itself, we are creating the world in every moment. Our life is our own creation. Realizing this is the first step towards *Radical Manifestation.*

Not Logical

The new paradigm makes very little sense to our logical mind, because our logic and reasoning is conditioned to think according to the structure of the old paradigm. Our attempts to explain it in the language of the current one is feeble, but it's the best we can do at this time.

It Works

Though we do have quantum physics to back up the new paradigm to an extraordinary degree, the only form of validation we have as an individual arises as a profound inner knowing — a subjective reality. Therefore, the metaphysical construction of reality is not so much a theory as an experience. The only proof of its value is that, when we trust it and go with it, it seems to work.

Radical Forgiveness

For me, of course, the best example of this is *Radical Forgiveness.* I have been teaching it for almost 10 years and find it to be extraordinarily successful. It really does work, and yet it is built entirely on the basis of the new metaphysical paradigm.

To the rational mind, raised in the context of the old objective paradigm, *Radical Forgiveness* makes no sense whatsoever. But even with an analytical, left-brained skeptic still operating from within the old paradigm, it works just as well — so long as he or she is willing to give it a try it by using the simple tools that the technology provides.

The Vest

Here's a story that proves that. I had only been doing workshops on *Radical Forgiveness* for a short while when one of the participants in a workshop I was doing in Australia told a story that was so heart-rending that I found myself unable to hold that it was perfect in the spiritual sense. She was in a state of despair about what was happening to her children and I was unable to bring her to a place of *Radical Forgiveness*. So I shared with the group that I could not hold it and was therefore unable to be their leader in any meaningful way. How could I expect them to apply the principle to their own problems if I was unable to apply it uniformly to all situations?

So I gave them two choices: (a) I would give them their money back, we would abandon the workshop and I would burn the book, or (b) we would go ahead with the workshop and do the processes even though none of us, including me, believed in it. Well, they chose the latter and we went ahead.

What was extraordinary was that by the end of the workshop, this person was in state of pure bliss and totally at peace with her situation. I know she still is to this day,

33

even though it was many years ago. The effect on the group and on me was profound. She gave me back my faith in the *Radical Forgiveness* process because if she could do it, given her story, anyone could.

After that we went on to another city, and in a week or so, a beautiful vest arrived in the mail that she had made for me. She said she had so much energy that night after the workshop, she had to put it into something. It was embroidered with all sorts of things out of the book.

Fig. 2. The Vest

I now wear this vest (or another one that she made subsequently), for at least one day of every workshop as testimony to two things. First, to remind me how fragile my own ability is in holding the context of perfection in the face of seemingly awful things happening, and second, as testimony to the fact that so long as you are willing to use the tools, it works anyway.

That incident proved that no belief of any kind is required for *Radical Forgiveness* to work. It has nothing to do with the intellectual mind; it is purely an energy experience. The tools provided simply enable the energy attached to certain wounds, thoughts, beliefs and assumptions, as well as situations, to flow where it needs to flow and to be dispersed. That's what makes *Radical Forgiveness* so fast and so easy to do.

Paradigms Clashing
I said earlier that neither logic nor even common sense determine where we are in the process of shifting between paradigms. Rather, that it just depends on the position you take at the time relative to your allegiance to one paradigm or the other.

Evolution versus Intelligent Design
Interestingly enough, we are, at the time of writing, witnessing in America the pure positionality of those who defend either one or the other of the two paradigms. One group maintains that Darwin's Theory of Evolution is the only valid explanation of how life began. The other group rejects Darwin's theory on the grounds that it cannot possibly explain the diversity, the complexity, symbiotic interdependence and sheer beauty of the life process. They have come up with a metaphysical notion called Intelligent Design to explain it. Their position is that nature can only be understood if we credit the design of it to some form of over-arching, albeit unknown intelligence.

Leaving aside the unfortunate fact that political conservatives have created a much perverted version of Intelligent

Design to stand as code for *creationism* (the idea that the world was created exactly according to the story in the Bible), and that their God was the designer, the pure idea of Intelligent Design nevertheless represents the view most closely associated with the metaphysical paradigm.

Oneness Versus Separateness

Similarly, another interesting split has occurred within the Christian Evangelical movement at the very moment I am writing this chapter, where the two factions are taking sides on the issue (as I see it), of oneness versus separateness.

The surface argument is about whether the government should be doing something about global warming or not. The debate is being framed in terms of one group asserting that human beings are above everything else in the great scheme of things and that their interests are paramount. Therefore, if cutting CO_2 emissions would be bad for the (American) economy and therefore bad for Americans, so the argument goes, that should take precedent over concern for the environment and climactic stability.

The other group is arguing that human beings should have concern for all of God's creation and that we should be good stewards of the planet and be responsible for it. Therefore we ought to do something about reducing emissions. It will be interesting to see how the debate unfolds, especially given the fact that the evangelicals as a group form a large part of George Bush's base and he is more of a mind to ignore global warming because to do anything about it would be bad for business.

Chapter 6
Living In Both Paradigms

At first blush, you would think that the two life paradigms were mutually exclusive. However, just as ordinary people, in taking more responsibility for their own health and healing, simply take the best of traditional medicine and the best of energy medicine and put them together into a combination that works for them, so we, as spiritual beings doing our spiritual journey on the earth plane, need to be able to work with both life paradigms at the same time. We need to be as much grounded in the paradigm based on the precepts of the objective construction of reality as we are in the one based on metaphysical and spiritual precepts.

I believe that we incarnate into the life experience in order to experience separation. The ultimate purpose of this is to magnify our sense of oneness by experiencing the opposite of it. Naturally, for this to work, it is necessary that we believe in separation, but once it has been experienced to the degree required according to our soul's assessment relative to what we agree to do prior to incarnating, we can begin the pre-determined process of waking up to the truth of who we are. *(This typically begins in mid-life for most people and may take several years.)* In effect, this process of awakening is the same thing as making the shift to the new paradigm.

The Default Paradigm

The above comments notwithstanding, it still holds true that in the Western world, when it comes to ordinary everyday life and practical matters, we mostly default to the objective reality paradigm for our construction of physical reality and life as we know it.

We can equate this with how, despite the fact that quantum physics has proven that Newtonian physics is fundamentally flawed, and despite the fact that quantum physics has been around now for more than half a century, we still default to Newtonian physics to help us understand the world in a practical way. It still works for us at that level.

We currently default to the old paradigm, at best, probably around 90 percent of the time. It keeps us grounded in the human experience in the same way that Newtonian physics keeps us grounded in everyday practical affairs. Only rarely do we reference quantum physics in our daily lives and in the same way, and only very occasionally are we able to see life from the perspective of the new paradigm.

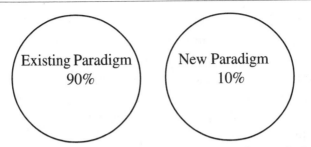

It would be all too easy to beat ourselves up for not being fully into the new paradigm and give up the process of transforming ourselves step by step or — worse — to kid ourselves that we are already there. We are not. Our consciousness is not evolved enough yet to be fully in it. But we are getting close. The ratio will change dramatically as a result of our mass awakening and transformation, but we must keep working at it.

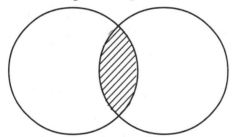

The task is to slowly but surely change the ratio between our being predominantly more in one or the other, and to arrive at the point where we can comfortably be in both at the same time.

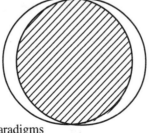

Fig. 3: Merging Paradigms

Practicing the Transition

It is not a case of waiting passively for this to happen. The tools of *Radical Forgiveness* and *Radical Manifestation* provide the opportunity to actually practice it. As you use the tools, you are in effect "faking it until you make it." But as we have already seen, since belief is not required, faking it will be very effective. You will actually experience both the transition and being in the new paradigm.

The RF/RM Bridge

Faking it when using the tools of *Radical Forgiveness* and *Radical Manifestation* enables us to suspend our normal way of thinking about life and be open to the new paradigm even before we fully understand it.

Each of the tools operates like a bridge between these two realities. They enable us to move freely and easily between them, almost without knowing it.

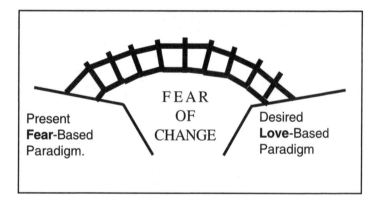

Fig. 4: The Bridge to Love

Like anything else, the more we practice something, the less fear we have about it. When the time comes for us to make the shift complete, we will be so accustomed to being in the vibration of the love-based reality (through using the tools) that our fears about making the final leap will have evaporated.

How long the transformation is going to take is anyone's guess. Obviously, it will vary from individual to individual, but to a large extent it will depend on how committed people are to using the tools that are available. *[These are listed in Appendix 1.]*

Remember, the tools are designed, not only to give us practice in being in the vibration of the metaphysical paradigm while we are manifesting, but to progressively and permanently raise our vibration to where we won't need them any more. By that time, our transformation will be complete and we will be fully empowered at all levels.

41

PART TWO

The Assumptions of Radical Manifestation

Chapter 7
Assumptions

In Part One it was necessary to establish that *Radical Manifestation* can only operate within the framework of the metaphysical paradigm. On that basis we are now able to outline the assumptions that form the foundation for *Radical Manifestation.*

Assumption #1. *Radical Manifestation arises from our realization that Spirit is the source of all our supply and that abundance is the natural condition of the Universe, there being no shortage of anything. It is from that place that we create and manifest what we desire knowing that we deserve to have anything we want.*

The one thing that most people would agree upon is that there is no shortage of energy in the Universe. There is an infinite supply of it. If everything of a physical nature is nothing more than energy made manifest through consciousness as quantum physics implies, (see the "wave" and "particle" theory on Page 32), then theoretically there should be no shortage of anything that we set our intention to have, assuming we know what it is we want and know how to ask for it.

Physicist David Bohm claims that the tangible reality of everyday life is really just an illusion, just like a holographic image. Beneath the so-called objective reality lies a deeper order of reality that continually gives birth to the material world. He called this level of reality the *implicate order* in which things which are not yet manifest are "enfolded," just waiting to made manifest or "unfolded" through the mechanism of consciousness. Once this has occurred, he refers to it as the *explicate order* of reality.

47

To Bohm, the manifestation of all form is simply the result of innumerable shifts between the implicate and explicate order of reality and that there is no limit to what can be made explicate out of the implicate order. It's all in there, enfolded in the implicate order in the form of energy, just waiting for us to bring it forth and make it explicate. We have the power to do so, and that's what I mean by *Radical Manifestation*. It's our choice to do it or not.

I doubt that you could claim never to have had the experience where you wanted something really badly and it inexplicably turned up just when you needed it! I defy anyone to say that it has never happened to them at least once in their life. I don't care if you interpreted it as a piece of luck or good fortune, or you could see an objective reason why it happened — your monkey mind will always invent something logical to explain something like that — but how about the possibility that you called it forth out of the implicate order?

If you think you are smarter than David Bohm, who is one of the most intelligent men on the planet, and your explanation is better than his, then *Radical Manifestation* may not be for you!

This brings me to the deservability issue that is hinted at in the last part of this first assumption. There are many core-negative beliefs that have arisen out of our adherence to the old paradigm, but the *"I am not worthy,"* and the *"I don't deserve,"* are among the worst. They all too effectively block our ability to manifest what we want out of

48

the field of abundance. They are incredibly disempowering and yet the vast majority of people have those beliefs and more like it. Such beliefs arise out of the extremely judgmental value system of the old paradigm.

The truth of the matter, however, is that the Universe is completely neutral. It does not judge anyone or anything and never engages in assessment of deservability or worthiness. It loves you unconditionally and gives you everything you ask for. The problem is that if you believe that you are undeserving, it will give you only what confirms your belief. You will only get what you think you deserve. As we said in Part One, if you want to know what your beliefs are, look at what is showing up in your life. There is a direct correlation.

> **Assumption #2** Radical Manifestation *depends upon the extent to which one is willing to clear from one's consciousness, using the* Radical Forgiveness *technology, any and all existing victim/perpetrator stories, along with any resentment, blame, expectation or judgments attached thereto.*

This is simply a matter of the quality and purity of your energy field and the level of your vibration. To be able manifest what you want in your life, you need your vibration to be fairly high and your energy field relatively clear.

Think of your energy field as being like the air filter in a car. The more clogged it is, the less efficient the engine can be. The more your energy field is clogged with resentment, anger, bitterness, sadness and the like, the lower your vibration will be and the less able you will be to practice *Radical Manifestation.*

Fortunately, you have at your disposal a technology that will enable you to clear your energy field of all the victim and perpetrator "stories" that carry a low vibration. That technology is *Radical Forgiveness.*

Early childhood wounds like abandonment, rejection, abuse, etc., will yield quickly to *Radical Forgiveness.* So will the pain of divorce, loss of a friend or spouse, betrayal, career problems and so on. (That's not to say that you don't allow yourself to have the feelings. You must do that. It is essential. Otherwise you will be doing a 'spiritual bypass,' and that does not work.) Guilt and shame will also yield quickly to *Radical Self-forgiveness.* (See Appendix for the On-line Self-Forgiveness Program.)

To have a high vibration, you must relinquish victim consciousness completely. Blame has no place in this paradigm. No more justifying and pointing the finger at others. You have to take responsibility for creating your own life — because the truth is that you do indeed create it.

What does it mean to have a high vibration? How can you tell whether a person has a high or low vibration? The following may help shed some light on this.

Low-Vibration People
People of low vibration tend to regularly experience emotions like anger, fear, resentment, jealousy, cynicism, apathy and other negative emotions. They tend to have a preponderance of core-negative beliefs. They tend to be energy vampires, taking more out of the system than they put in. They have tendency to lay blame and justify.

High-Vibration People
Someone with a high vibration is likely to be free of most negative emotions and will have a predominance of core-positive beliefs. He or she is likely to be bright, happy, open-minded, likable, clear, cooperative and creative. High-vibration people are more apt to experience emotions like appreciation, gratitude, compassion, humility and

love than those of a more negative nature. They are more likely to draw on the finer energy coming from Spirit and eschew energy that emanates from Ego. People of high vibration usually have high integrity. High-vibration people tend to put a lot more into a system than they take out. They give energy to those around them rather than seek to draw it from others. It feels good to be in their presence.

A Vibratory Scale

The chart below outlines a model of how individual qualities of mind rank in terms of vibration. This information is taken from the work of David Hawkins, M.D., Ph.D., and his ground-breaking book, *Power vs. Force,* in which he has logged, in rank order, how each quality of mind scores on a scale of one to 600.

Quality	Log	Emotion
Peace	600	Bliss
Joy	540	Serenity
Love	500	Reverence
Reason	400	Understanding
Acceptance	**350**	**Forgiveness**
Willingness	**310**	**Optimism**
Neutrality	250	Trust
Courage	200	Affirmation
Pride	175	Scorn
Anger	150	Hate
Desire	125	Craving
Fear	100	Anxiety
Grief	75	Regret
Apathy	50	Despair
Guilt	30	Blame
Shame	20	Humiliation

Fig. 5: Scale of Consciousness

200 — The Pivot Point

The critical point on the scale is the 200 mark. At less than 200, the person's main concern is personal survival, and they tend to take more out of a system than they put in. Their effect on the overall energy field of any group they are a part of is liable, therefore, to be net-negative. Someone above the 200 mark is more likely to begin to consider the welfare of others as well as his or her own, and are likely, therefore, to have a net-positive effect on the overall energy field of the group.

To put this in perspective, Hawkins points out that the vast majority of the world's population is well below the 200 mark. However, because the few people vibrating at very high levels (500+) are counteracting the energy of the majority vibrating below 200, the average is 207. Only in the last decade has it passed the 200 mark. Someone vibrating at around 350 is counteracting 200,000 people below 200. Someone vibrating at the level of 500 is counteracting 750,000 people below 200.

Not Good or Bad

The idea is not to judge anyone as less than or better than someone else, or as good or bad. As Hawkins says:

> "Moralistic judgments are merely a function of the viewpoint from which they proceed. We see, for instance, that a person in Grief, which calibrates at a low level of 75, will be in a much better condition if he rises to Anger, which calibrates at 150. Anger, itself a destructive emotion, is still a low state of conscious-

ness, but as social history shows, apathy can imprison entire subcultures as well as individuals. If the hopeless can come to want something better (Desire — 125) and use the energy of Anger at 150 to develop Pride (175), they may then be able to take the step to Courage which calibrates at 200, and proceed to improve their individual or collective conditions."

Shoot For 350-500

I have consistently stressed willingness in this book and in all my writings on *Radical Forgiveness*. Because willingness enters at 310 and acceptance at 350, I had earlier concluded that 400 would be the vibratory level people would need to reach to be fully aligned with, and living from, the paradigm that fully supported the *Radical Forgiveness* and *Radical Manifestation* technology.

However, on closer reading of Hawkins' works, I am now persuaded that a vibratory rate of 500 is a more appropriate goal, at least for the advanced program (see next page), especially given that we are now adding *Radical Manifestation* to *Radical Forgiveness*. It is also the point at which Hawkins says spiritual awareness takes a giant leap. To quote Hawkins —

"On our scale of consciousness, there are two critical points that allow for major advancement. The first is at 200, the initial level of empowerment: Here the willingness to stop blaming and accept responsibility of one's own actions, feeling, and beliefs arises. (As long as cause and responsibility are projected outside of oneself, one will remain in the powerless mode of victimhood.) The second is the 500 level, which is reached by <u>accepting love and non-judgmental forgiveness as a life-style,</u> exercising unconditional kindness to all persons, things and events *without exception*." (His italics.)

From this we can see that to be anywhere on the scale between 200 and 500 would be good in terms of being willing to give up the "blame-game" and be responsible for one's own life, but it is not until we reach 500 that *Radical Manifestation* becomes so deeply anchored in our consciousness that it becomes our default life-style.

My sense of it also is that it is only when we begin to consistently vibrate at around 500 that we would come into our full power as conscious manifestors of our own desired reality. It seems reasonable to suppose that one cannot begin living the metaphysical paradigm if one's vibration is less than 350. That's why doing the *Radical Forgiveness* work which will get us beyond 350, is a prerequisite for getting to full *Radical Empowerment* at around 500.

For many of us, it might be that we would vacillate between 350 and 500, depending on what is happening in our lives at the time, perhaps only reaching 500 in rare moments. Nevertheless, it remains that 500 seems to be the right goal to aim for in our advanced *Radical Empowerment* program, which is why it is called the "500 Club Program." (See Appendix.)

Assumption #3 *Radical Manifestation arises in direct proportion to one's willingness to live in the metaphysical paradigm, aligning one's values, beliefs and behaviors with it, at least to the extent that is possible at this time.*

In Part One we laid out the underlying values, beliefs, concepts, ideas, and assumptions associated with the paradigm we have called the metaphysical construction of reality, so there is no need to repeat them here.

We also said that shifting from the one paradigm to the other was necessarily a gradual process and that *willingness* is the key. As long as one is willing and uses whatever means possible to make the transition and raise one's vibration as indicated in the last chapter, that is enough.

That would include, of course, using all the tools of *Radical Forgiveness* on a consistent basis and making that a habit. As we have seen, being genuinely willing to abide by the values and beliefs of the new paradigm will raise your vibration sufficient to enable you to be the manifestor you aspire to be.

It is also important that we remain fully grounded in the actual human experience. The danger in identifying too strongly with the new paradigm, with its emphasis on spirituality, is that we might forget that the human experience is an "in-body" one. It is to be experienced primarily through our senses and mediated through our feelings. It is an exercise in living in both the World of Humanity and the World of Divine Truth simultaneously. Briefly, these can be described as follows:

The World of Humanity represents the world of objective reality we see as *outside ourselves*. As a world of form, it provides the setting in which we live our everyday human lives, as well as the reality we experience through our five senses. It holds the energy patterns of death, change, fear, limitation, and duality. This world provides us with the environment in which we, as spiritual beings, can experience being human.

The World of Divine Truth, on the other hand, has no physical form and already carries the energy pattern of eternal life, infinite abundance, love, and oneness with Spirit. Even though we cannot perceive this world with our senses, and we scarcely possess the mental capacity to comprehend it, we can get enough of a sense of it to know that it is real. Such activities as prayer, meditation and *Radical Forgiveness*, all of which raise our vibration, allow us to access the World of Divine Truth.

These *existential realms* differ not in terms of place or time but solely in their vibrational level. The study of quantum physics has proven that all reality consists of energy patterns and that consciousness sustains these energy patterns. Thus, the world of form exists as dense concentrations of energy vibrating at frequencies we can experience through our physical senses. On the other

58

hand, we experience the World of Divine Truth as an inner knowing and an extrasensory awareness.

Because these two worlds exist on the same continuum, we do not live sometimes in one and sometimes in the other. We live in both worlds at the same time. However, which world we experience at any given moment depends upon our awareness of them. Obviously, as human beings our consciousness resonates easily with the World of Humanity. Our senses naturally pull us into that world and convince us that it is real. As we saw on Page 39, our task is to learn to be in both worlds at the same time.

> **Assumption #4.** Radical Manifestation *as manifestation depends on one's clarity in knowing what one wants and why one wants it, how clearly the request is made, how much gratitude can be felt knowing that it is already done, and finally, on one's willingness to drop one's attachment to having it.*

The are a number of issues imbedded in this assumption and they all need to be addressed.

The first, most obvious thing to point out is that the Universe will not give you what you want unless you ask. It probably knows, of course, but since you have free will it will only respond to a request. Therefore, you must know what you want and you must find a way to express it in very clear terms.

Be careful what you ask for, though. In our materialistic culture we have been taught to use the power of our mind to set and achieve goals that are purely materialistic in nature and without much reference to higher-order spiritual values. Such goals are often driven by non-spiritual, low consciousness values such as greed, envy, competition, control, fear, need to succeed, need for approval and all other forms of extrinsic motivations that have their origins in the idea of scarcity and fear-based values.

There is nothing intrinsically wrong or bad about materialistic goals, but we need to realize that if driven by these

kinds of values they will not result in happiness or satisfaction, either for oneself or for the collective as a whole.
In fact, there is a distinct possibility that such goals create
harm, or at the very least, dissatisfaction or disappointment.

The other trap that we fall into by having goals based on
low consciousness values is attachment to outcome. If
the goals are not reached we feel that we have failed. That's
because we have the belief that we ourselves, or our Ego,
are the ones who are doing it, not Spirit.

The answer is to set materialistic intentions that have specific reference to higher goals and associated values.

The Three Levels of Intention:

1. Spiritual Intentions
Examples of this type of goal might be peace, happiness, oneness, abundance, joy of giving and receiving,
freedom and being of service. The attributes they would
lead you to have are such things as unconditionality,
non-attachment, surrender, gratitude, generosity, love
and joy. The end state that such goals lead to is Divine
consciousness and a desire to connect to Source.

2. Transformational Intentions
These are goals that arise out of a desire for personal
transformation and growth to reach the state of awakening consciousness. Examples might be to awaken,
to know our purpose and mission, to find a level of

real appreciation and acceptance of what is, willingness to forgive and ability to let go, to serve others, to connect with Spirit, etc. The attributes these goals would lead you towards would be compassion, trust, forgiveness, humility, openness and conviction. In meeting these goals you would experience synchronicity, insight, epiphany, and heightened awareness.

3. Baseline Intentions or Materialistic Goals
These are desires rooted in the material world. Examples might be physical comfort, wealth, material goods, freedom to act, good health, respect, status, success, power, control, recognition, etc. The attributes these lead to are material success, pride, practical knowledge, groundedness and health. The values at this baseline level are likely to be physical survival, comfort, recognition and material success.

Refer Upwards
Each level should reference the one above it. In other words, when you give a reason why you wish to manifest something material, the reason should come at least from the transformational level, or even the inspirational level, but not just from the baseline level. In that way, you invoke the values of those higher levels to drive the practical or materialistic goals, thereby giving your goals a higher vibration. Also, as we have already said, the importance of your attaching the feelings associated with already having that which you want is of paramount importance, but what is even more important is that the emotions should be attached to the higher level intentions, not the lower ones.

Let me give you a down-to-earth example from my own life.

When I was growing up I always loved the Jaguar as a car, but always saw it as a car that was for the well-to-do and successful business people. My father was an aircraft technician and rode a bike seven miles to work and back every day and we didn't have a car. Not until he was into his fifties did he own a car and even then it was only a Mini. We were definitely working class people living in England, which is a class-based society. It is not as easy to overcome your class origins in England as it is in America. Money alone doesn't do it.

To me, the Jaguar seemed like a car for people of a different class or for people who had made it in life. It represented success and an affluent life-style as well as class. Jaguar people were definitely upper class. I was not.

Fig. 6: The Jaguar

To set myself the goal of having a Jaguar would therefore be a baseline goal. It was unashamably materialistic, but I referenced my intention to create a Jaguar to a transformational goal of overcoming my poverty consciousness and my inferior class consciousness so I could push through to a new level of business success. That is another baseline goal, but it actually references an inspirational goal of being able to be of service to more people and achieving my mission of creating a world of forgiveness by 2012. That is my work and therefore my business.

Cars in general mean very little to me. They are just a form of transport, and I don't relate to them as status symbols based on their price. In fact, I had owned a vehicle prior to the Jag which was much more expensive. But it held no meaning for me. It was just a vehicle to get around in. However, I gave the Jag a meaning that supported my own personal transformation and referenced my divine purpose.

So, the point here is make sure that you have some higher level goals to give a reference to your baseline goals. And they must be real and authentic. It's no good making them up. If you really can't find reasons for having something in terms of either your own transformation or divine purpose, then you should question whether it is worth putting energy into manifesting them at all, assuming there is no real and genuine need. What we see so much of today is people accumulating "stuff" for the sake of having it and feeling ever more dissatisfied. The reason they feel this way is because it is devoid of meaning.

The worst scenario is to reverse the process and set higher level goals with the real intention of satisfying baseline goals. An example might be tithing 10 percent of your income not so much out of your desire to give back to your Source as an expression of your gratitude, but out of the expectation that you will get more money in return. If you try to manipulate the Universe in this way, you will receive some interesting lessons in integrity.

The last part of this assumption is probably the most important and yet the most difficult. In the same way that *Radical Forgiveness* is about coming to the realization that there is nothing to forgive, so *Radical Manifestation* is about giving up any attachment to receiving what you asked for.

Yes, it is important to put a lot of energy into your intention and to feel it as intensely as possible — but then you must let it go completely. If it doesn't manifest, it doesn't mean that you have failed. It just means that your spiritual intelligence has decided that either something else better awaits you, the time is not right, or you're not ready to receive it yet.

PART THREE

Mind Training
And Spiritual Practice
For *Radical Manifestation*

RADICAL MANIFESTATION

Chapter 8
The Mind

This is by no means the only book or program on the market that promises to show you how to manifest your dreams. However, most of them depend on giving you techniques that train you to override the long-term programming of your subconscious and unconscious minds.

Even though that approach has been around for a long time, beginning perhaps with Napoleon Hill's famous book, *Think and Grow Rich,* it is worth looking at why that approach is seldom successful or at least only successful to a certain point. Then we can look at the approach taken in this book and understand the difference.

It will be helpful to first look at how the mind actually works and discover why our programming is so resistant to change.

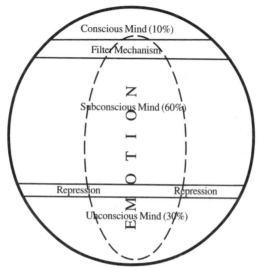

Fig. 7: The Mind

As you will see from the diagram above, there are three areas of mind — plus the emotional component which covers all three.

1. The Conscious Mind

This is that part of the mind from which we operate with conscious awareness. It is responsible for our day-to-day cognitive activity. It is thought to be no more than 10 percent of our total mental activity.

2. The Subconscious Mind

The subconscious is one level down from the conscious mind. It is that part of our mind which stores all of our learned ideas, beliefs, attitudes, prejudices and habits as well as many of our basic needs and drives. It is programmable, but once the program is in, it is very resistant to change. It is said that the subconscious mind is 90 percent programmed by the time we are seven or eight years old and that, consequently, our life script has been written by that time.

The cellular biologist Dr. Bruce Lipton, author of *The Biology of Belief,* says the conscious mind is a 40-bit-per-second processor that handles about five percent of our operations, whereas the subconscious mind is a 40-million-bit-per-second processor that handles 95 percent of our operations.

The content of the subconscious mind is always manifesting itself as observable behavior. It continually emanates creative energy that, due to the law of attraction, creates actual situations in one's own life experience. That's why we say that if you want to know what your beliefs are, see what turns up in your life. In other words, your life is a mirror of what exists in your subconscious mind.

3. The Unconscious Mind
This is a level which goes deeper than the subconscious. The content is much more difficult to recognize or to access. Repressed unconscious material is buried way down below the level of awareness and is seldom made manifest as recognizable behavior.

That's because the content of this part of the mind is surrounded by sophisticated defense mechanisms that keep everything hidden and deeply repressed. It's not that it doesn't result in behavior; it does. But it is extremely well camouflaged.

71

Our deepest fears, held shame and most painful wounds lie buried and unresolved in this part of our mind. Our most strongly held resentments remain shackled down here along with our unresolved grief and profound self-hatred. The unconscious mind is the repository of dark secrets we just can't bear to look at and base desires that we can't own. It is a dark place. It is constantly emanating energy, and its effects, though hardly recognizable and seldom, if ever, correctly understood for what causes them, are powerful indeed. The potential that such energy carries for creating all sorts of mischief is enormous.

It is also interesting to see how these three aspects of mind are structured in layers and how both the subconscious and unconscious parts of the mind each have a built-in system of self-preservation. In particular, there is a mechanism that operates between the conscious mind and the subconscious mind that blocks and filters information flowing in both directions.

Verification
This filter mechanism also acts as a verification system in the sense that, if an idea occurs in the conscious mind such as *"I am wealthy now,"* the filter mechanism dives down into the subconscious and unconscious parts of the mind to check whether the idea is in alignment with what already exists down there. If it finds, for example, that there is a pre-existing idea, belief system or attitudinal complex that says something like *"you are not of the right class to be wealthy,"* or *"money is bad and only bad people are rich,"* the idea will be rejected.

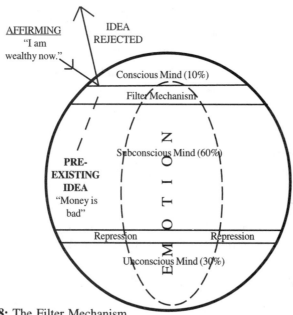

Fig. 8: The Filter Mechanism

Blocking Mechanisms

The conscious mind is comparatively weak and unable to override the subconscious mind. Therefore, in this example, the truth is that a person who appears on the face of it to consciously want more money, really does not. He or she will, therefore, find ways to sabotage any flow of money in his direction. This is a very common phenomenon and, of course, is an example of how the subconscious and unconscious mind blocks our ability to manifest what we want.

The current paradigm of reality that we work with now has loaded our collective subconscious mind with all manner of beliefs that get in the way of our power to create

73

whatever we want — health, money, freedom, love, ful-fillment and so on. This is a process that has been going on for centuries, so it is not going to change quickly and we are fooling ourselves if we think we can simply over-ride our subconscious and unconscious minds by mouth-ing a few affirmations and making conscious resolutions. In order to reprogram ourselves to be in alignment with our true creative power that the metaphysical paradigm tells us we have, we must do two things:

1. Effectively bypass the parts of our subconscious and unconscious minds that hold all the old programming and employ instead our spiritual intelligence.

2. Use certain attributes of the subconscious and un-conscious minds to start the process off, but hand it over entirely to our spiritual intelligence well before the negative programming kicks in.

Most programs focus almost entirely on the use of the mind and, since they are primarily grounded in the old paradigm, offer no awareness about spiritual intelligence. The approach taken in this book is grounded in the meta-physical paradigm, so its main focus is not on mind train-ing but on spiritual practice.

Whereas mental intelligence is connected to the intellec-tual part of the mind, known as the prefrontal cortex, and while emotional intelligence is located in the limbic brain, spiritual intelligence resides in the heart. It's the intelli-gence of our soul.

Unlike the other two forms of intelligence which are fully individualized, spiritual intelligence is a shared phenomenon. It is part of the larger collective spiritual intelligence and group soul. It is directly connected to Universal Intelligence. Most of what we need to learn in the way of technique for *Radical Manifestation* is directed at this part of our consciousness.

That said, however, insofar as the manifestation process starts off in the mental mind as an idea or a vision and is initially propelled by a desire (emotion), then it makes sense to involve both mental and emotional intelligence in the manifestation process, at least at the beginning.

The idea is to use the mental minds (conscious, subconscious and unconscious) to jump start the process prior to handing it over to spiritual intelligence, making sure that we hand it over well before the negative programming kicks in. We can use well-established techniques like the power of suggestion, visualization techniques and emotional leverage to supercharge the process before giving it over to Spirit.

We can formalize this into six steps in the manifestation process, which I will describe in the following chapter.

Chapter 9
Six Steps to Manifestation

The process of manifestation can be broken down into six distinct steps. The first four occur as mental and emotional phenomena. The last two arise out of spiritual practice and are the most difficult to master. They are nevertheless the most important.

1. Become aware of the need.
2. Clarify and give precise language to the idea.
3. Visualize the end result.
4. Feel the emotions of already receiving it.
5. Hand it over completely to Spirit.
6. Drop all attachment to having it.

Step #1
Becoming Aware of the Need

This awareness arises either as a consequence of an inner (intrinsic) longing for something or is the result of some outside (extrinsic) message or event.

Assuming that all our basic needs for food, shelter and safety are met, it is probably true to say that those of an intrinsic nature are more likely to be longings for things associated with the inspirational or transformational goals, whereas the more extrinsic kinds of triggers are more likely to be for baseline goals.

Relative Deprivation

Advertising and all other forms of marketing are designed to create an awareness of some baseline need, more often than not one that we didn't even know we had. They do this by creating in you a feeling of relative deprivation. No matter how much "stuff" you have already, marketers try to make you feel deprived on the basis that others have things you don't have, or they have the latest version and you don't.

Being the Observer

The important part of this step is developing an awareness of the awareness of need arising in you. This is why your "observer" is crucial. The observer is that part of you that watches you from a non-judgmental, neutral place apart from you. It is more that your own self-awareness; it is part of your Higher, 'I AM' Self.

Bearing in mind that the messages you are bombarded with every day are aimed at your subconscious mind against which there is little defence, it is very important to be able to stand apart and watch your reactions. Also, to notice when and how you are triggered, and how you get hooked. The objective, however, is not to make this wrong or to judge your desires in any way. If you like to stay in fashion and have the latest clothes, or keep up with the latest gadgets, then why not? Who says that you shouldn't set a goal to manifest an expensive leather coat or have the latest computer?

What Level of Intention?

The key, however, is to have an awareness of your longings and where they come from. It really helps to be able to classify your desire in terms of the three levels of intention mentioned earlier. Is it simply a baseline intention to create something of a material nature? Does it arise out of a desire to transform yourself? Is it coming as a longing for meaning, purpose and fulfillment? Is it a combination of two or three of these intentions?

This is not to say that a desire for something that is simply materialistic is bad. There's nothing wrong with wanting things. But we should clearly understand that, unless it references one or more of the levels above it, it won't do a lot for us. Material things don't lead to happiness or fulfillment, and by themselves, they give little meaning to our lives. As long as we know that and don't kid ourselves that the new car is the answer to our low self-esteem or depression, then what's wrong with having a nice car? Why wouldn't the Universe want to give it to us? Go for it, I say! But be aware.

Evaluating the Need

What is important then, before moving on to the second step, is to be able to examine, without judgment, our wants, our desires and our longings to see if they are real; to assess whether they are important or just frivolous; to notice whether they have meaning or value to us or represent merely a passing fancy. It doesn't matter either way, so long as you know and you are not deluding yourself.

Ask Why?
A helpful question to ask is "why?" Why do I want this? What will it lead to? What good would it do? What's the payoff?

The "why" question is important from a technical standpoint also. Remember, even though we have to ensure that the programming that is already in the subconscious mind doesn't cancel our intention to have what we want before we have handed it over to Spirit, we are still employing that part of the mind in the process of manifestation.

What we know about the subconscious mind is that it is less likely to block something, even if it contradicts what it already knows, if you give it a reason or an excuse. That's why all the manifestation tools and processes ask that you give reasons for wanting the thing that you desire.

Since it does take energy and effort to manifest something, you have to ask whether it is worth expending energy in manifesting this thing. That means setting some kind of priority. What is most important to you? What is most meaningful? What would lead to the most peace, happiness and joy? Again, reference it to the higher intentions.

80

Step #2:
Clarify and Give Precise
Language to the Idea.

Having become aware of the desire, it is now important that you get very clear about precisely what you are asking the Universe to provide for you. You may already have done some of this in asking yourself some of the questions in Step One, but there are some guidelines about how to articulate or give word to what you want.

Clarity

This can range from something as non-specific as *"I need help,"* to something so detailed and specific that it even includes a very precise list of the attributes it should have. Even though one is precise and the other is open, there is nevertheless clarity in both approaches.

The point is to be clear and unambiguous about what you intend to create and how open you are to having it show up in any form the Universe decides to present it in. Clearly, an *"I need help,"* statement means "I'll take help in any form." On the other hand, if there is a detail that is important it should be included, especially if that is the one thing that gives your intention meaning at the second and third levels.

Returning to my own example of the Jaguar car, not only did I hold an intention to have a Jaguar in order to transform my consciousness about social class, worthiness and success, but it had to be a particular model. The S-type is

81

very reminiscent of the 50s Mark 1 model to which I had attached that particular meaning, so no other model would have done; not even the more expensive XJ model. I had to have clarity in my intention with regard to that detail or the whole point of having the car would have been lost.

The List

In the 80's and 90's it became very common for people who were looking for a mate to make a very detailed list of the attributes they wanted in a mate. I had a friend who did this and someone showed up who seemed to be the answer to her prayer in every respect. They got married but soon after she realized that she had asked for all the right things but forgot to make it a requirement that she should be able to love him! They divorced soon after.

The Power of the Word

Once you know what you want and have become very clear about it in your own mind, you must give it word. Whenever you speak something you give it power. Words have enormous energy behind them and they are power-fully creative, especially if they are accompanied by emotional energy, so make sure you use emotional words in your statement that evoke feeling.

By all means write your intentions down very clearly, making sure that you have all the details covered, but once you have done that, read it out loud. That is extremely important. It is even more powerful to read it to someone else, or even better, a group of people, so long as they are aligned with you in consciousness. Other people so aligned can magnify the energy quite significantly.

Always Present Tense

The subconscious mind has no concept of future. It operates only in the present. Therefore we must always speak or write everything in the present tense, even if what we say sounds awkward or is grammatically incorrect. Never say, *"I will enjoy having ......"* Instead you say, *"I am enjoying having ...."*

Already Done

For similar reasons, you need to speak of your intention as already done and received. If you say, "I want something," you are giving power to the word, "want." You will therefore continue to get the result of the word you have empowered — want. Therefore, you must say that you "have" something now. *"It is done."*

This is not simply a question of fooling the subconscious mind. It is the absolute truth that it's already done. There is no past or future to be concerned with. There is only this moment and as soon as you speak the word, you make explicate what is already in the implicate order. That's why it is a good idea to say after stating your intention - *"and so it is,"* or, *"it is done."* By saying that, you are aligning with the metaphysical paradigm of reality and with what your spiritual intelligence knows to be the truth.

Give it a Time Limit

Having just said that time is not a factor, there is good reason why you would always want to include a time scale in your statement of intention. Though there is no actual lag between something being enfolded in the great sea of infinite possibility and its coming into material existence, our spiritual intelligence probably has no awareness of time either. So it might be oblivious to the idea of "when." If we include it in our statement of intent, it will hear us.

Be careful, though, to ensure that in giving some sort of *"by such and such a time...."* statement you don't reinforce the idea of future and move the writing out of present tense. That's when the grammar is likely to get weird. For example: *"I have found my perfect line of work and am feeling great joy because it is before the end of next month,"* or, *"I am joyfully finding my perfect line of work now, well before the end of this year."*

Step #3
Visualizing the End Result

While words are powerful, it is also true that a picture is worth a thousand words. Forming a picture in your mind of what you intend is another way of getting clarity and is helpful in that regard. More importantly, however, building a picture in your mind is another way of saying that it is done, especially if it helps you activate the emotions you would feel when the real thing shows up. Athletes know this well. They always rehearse a perfect performance in their minds before they go out to perform.

So make sure when you build your picture that you include in it elements that give it a "now" meaning, not a future meaning. The picture should say "it is happening now."

You can also increase the power of the picture by enlarging it to an enormous size, taking up the whole sky even. Be your own cinematographer by zooming in on the most important symbols in the picture. Give it sound as well and make those sounds good and loud. Make it a rousing performance with as much kinesthetic, visual and aural stimulation as possible.

There are people who say that they cannot visualize easily. What they actually mean is that they cannot mentally construct a new image very easily. If I ask people to visualize their car, their house, or their child's face, they have no trouble at all accessing their visual memory. Once they have done that, then I ask them to imagine the new thing. That usually solves the problem. It seems that for some people imagining something is easier than trying to visualize it.

Step #4
Feel the Emotions of Already Receiving It

Recent books on the power of prayer, most notably one by Gregg Braden entitled *The Isaiah Effect,* have proven that emotion is the key element. Not just feelings like the excitement of anticipation and expectation stressed by the early pioneers of positive thinking, but the feelings that arise when what is asked for actually arrives. Joy, thankfulness, appreciation, gratitude, wonder and awe.

When the manifestation process begins to work and you start getting what you ask for, these emotions will become more intense and more frequently experienced. You will cry tears of joy and thankfulness because you will begin to realize how much you are loved. You will feel so blessed by the Universe as it showers its abundance onto you. You will be overcome with gratitude.

In the beginning though, when you are just beginning to work with *Radical Empowerment* and *Radical Manifestation*, you will have to work at generating those feelings. You will have to imagine how you will feel under such circumstances and do your best to move into those feelings for real. One way to do this is to find an incident in your memory of having felt this way, even if only for an instant. Focus on that memory of the feeling and let it grow within you. Once the neuropeptides associated with that feeling start flowing in your body, you can simply transfer that feeling to that which you are visualizing in the moment and anchor in to that.

Frankly, these feelings will occur at a much more profound level with second and third level intentions than with baseline intentions. The higher level intentions tend to satisfy desires for things like happiness, peace, harmony, freedom, joy and acceptance. Intentions created around material goals tend to generate feelings more associated with our lower nature, such as excitement, expectation and the satisfaction of the desires like greed, avarice, need for status, power, acceptance and so on.

What is important here is that you attach the feelings to the words that you use to articulate the intention (Step 2).

The effect of this is to strongly reinforce the idea that what you have asked for has been given you already. I am sure you have grasped by now the importance of that principle.

Step #5
Hand it Over Completely to Spirit

What we have done up to now with the first four steps might be helpful to anyone working from either the old paradigm or the new one, but from here on the process definitely depends on a willingness to work under the assumptions of the metaphysical paradigm to the exclusion of the other one. This is also the part where *Radical Manifestation* becomes a matter of spiritual practice rather than mental gymnastics.

A Higher Authority
It is where we say thank you to our subconscious mind for supporting us thus far, but from this point on, we refuse to accept from it any further involvement. Whatever chatter the subconscious or unconscious mind puts forth from now on, we pay no attention to whatsoever. We are now working with, and deferring to, a higher authority and we access it not through our mind but through our spiritual intelligence.

Who's in Control?
The first level of our spiritual practice lies in coming to understand that it is not our game; we (our egos) are not in control and we have little or no idea what's going on. Our Higher Self (Soul) is in control and it is only that part

of us that understands how life works and knows what the Divine plan is for us, both individually and collectively.

Humility

Surrender is what this step is all about, and humility is the pre-requisite. Having put quite a bit of energy into determining our intentions, clarifying them, articulating them and feeling the emotions, the task now is to give it over entirely to one's Higher Self and surrender it to Spirit. Only it knows what is best for us.

Co-creation

However, we must be careful here. This is not a recipe for apathy, inaction or a fatalistic attitude. We don't just do nothing and leave it to Spirit to take care of everything. The principle here is co-creation, not dependence. Each one of us is part of Spirit — little bits of "God Stuff," if you will. God is within all of us, so in order to expand our own consciousness and that of the God within, we are responsible for co-creating every aspect of our lives with God.

Paradox

Once again we find ourselves in the same kind of paradoxical situation that we seem to continually find ourselves in when working with the metaphysical paradigm. At the same time as we are asked surrender it all to Spirit, God, Universal Intelligence or whatever other name you want to give to the Source, we must nevertheless remain responsible and accountable for creating our own lives.

Goal Setting

Another conundrum relating to this paradox arises whenever we talk about goal setting, even in the context of *Radical Empowerment* and *Radical Manifestation*. The conundrum is this: If everything is perfect just the way it is, what is the point of setting a goal?

If I am at point A, and I set a goal to get to point B, then am I not making an assumption that A is not OK and that B is more OK than A? Otherwise, why bother?

By this logic, goal-setting is going against one of the principles of the metaphysical paradigm. However, there is another aspect to the paradigm that says that human beings will always engage in activities like goal-setting simply in order to learn that B is no better than A and that the only point of making the journey from A to B is what one learns (C) on the way.

Buckminster Fuller used a scientific word to describe this situation. The word was "precession."

Precession

It is not an easy concept to explain, but imagine that you are sitting on a chair that swivels and you are holding between your two hands in front of you a spinning bicycle wheel. If you try to tilt the wheel to the left or right, it will cause you to begin to swivel the chair you are sitting on. In other words, the force you apply to the axis of the wheel is resisted, but the reaction is delayed such that it occurs at a point 90 degrees later in its rotation. Similarly, if you push a spinning top to the right, it will move forward (assuming the top is spinning counter-clockwise). Gyroscopes use the same principle and are used as compasses in aircraft.

It doesn't matter if you understand the theory of precession or not. The point is that when things are put into motion in one direction and certain forces are applied to the moving object, other (perhaps unexpected) movements occur. In this case, the results come at 90 degrees to the direction of motion.

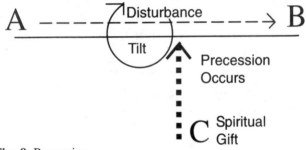

A - - - - - Disturbance - - - - → B

Tilt

Precession
Occurs

C Spiritual
Gift

Fig: 9. Precession

Fuller used this analogy to point out that it is necessary to be in motion — proceeding from point A to point B — for there to be any unexpected spiritual outcome (C) entering in from 90 degrees to the direction being travelled. Furthermore, it is necessary that some force be applied of a kind that is intended to upset the equilibrium of the moving object (you), before the change can occur.

Begin the Journey
So, the idea is that you set an intention to go from A to B, simply to be in motion or to be on a journey. You aim for

B because that is all you know. Your awareness of the big picture is too limited to be aware of C which is really what the journey is all about. It comes in at 90 degrees to the direction of your travel and occurs only when you experience some kind of disturbance to your equilibrium. Whereas B might be a baseline goal, C would almost certainly be one related to transformation (level 2) or inspiration (level 3).

Trusting the Process
In terms of the actual process, setting out from A to get to B equates to the first four steps. Not knowing what C is, when it might come in, or what it might look like, all the while knowing that something other than B might be given — or nothing at all, equates to Steps Five and Six.

Step #6
Dropping All Attachment to Having It

This is the hardest step of all. Having spent a lot of energy generating desire and commitment, feeling the joy and gratitude of having it, creating the certainty of knowing that an abundant Universe wants to bless you with it, you then have to give up your need to have it. Bummer! That's really hard.

It helps to refer back to Fuller's precession model and drop our attachment to B, knowing that C might be on the way and it might be better than B. But that's a trap too, because we are substituting one attachment for another. Instead of being attached to B, we are now attached to C.

We might as well admit it, this one is virtually beyond our capacity as a human being to achieve. Step Five is hard enough, but this is almost impossible. But remember, we only have to be *willing* to drop our attachment to having it. So, let that be the practice. Keep telling yourself that you are willing to have no attachment to having it.

What you can do, though, is to continue to match the high vibration of willingness with other feelings, thoughts and actions that carry at least as high a vibration. Stay energized and enthusiastic about your vision, knowing the Universe has heard your request and is working on giving you that or better. And don't confuse non-attachment with resignation or being disconnected. Letting go is not 'giving up.'

You will know the difference between non-attachment and the lower vibration qualities like resignation by how you feel. The lower the vibration, the more negative you will feel. Being in the space of willingness to be without attachment will give you a feeling of excitement, openness, and anticipation of being abundantly supplied in whatever way the Universe decides is best for you.

Chapter 10
Ways to Sabotage Yourself

W e need to keep reminding ourselves that the Universe is a place of total abundance and that being able to manifest is nothing out of the ordinary. We can be secure in knowing that quantum physics shows it to be a perfectly natural phenomenon. The only thing that blocks our ability to manifest freely is our commitment to a belief system that doubts that this is so. Then, in order to prove ourselves right, we subconsciously arrange to sabotage our ability to manifest. Here are a few ways that we do this that you might want to watch out for.

1. Fixating on B and missing C
As discussed in the previous chapter, the real purpose of setting a goal (B) is to give you something to move towards from (A), so that you are in motion long enough to encounter (C). However, we can become so intent on getting to (B) that we fail to notice (C). Whereas (B) is gross energy and perhaps already in manifest form, (C) is

usually very subtle, latent and, at times, no more than a potentiality. If we are too fixated on (B), we will miss the subtle signs and messages that (C) uses to catch our attention and we might then miss the opportunity, or fail to generate the intent, to bring it into form.

So, be sure to stay alive to subtle signs and messages that seem to be coming in at 90 degrees and check them out to see if they have meaning. Be discerning, of course — skeptical even. You don't want to be seeing every little thing that happens as some kind of sign. A good rule of thumb is that if something occurs three times and you feel that the connection between you and those events is too strong to ignore, then you might want to explore it further.

2) Pursuing (B) Halfheartedly

The opposite side of this same coin is being halfhearted about pursuing (B). If we don't bring much energy to the journey then there's not much juice from which to create (C). We have to give Spirit something to work with. Put 100 percent intention into creating (B) while remaining open to what might want to come in from the side.

3) Chickening Out

Having spent our whole life believing in a paradigm that not only worked but seemed self-evidently true, it is very difficult to put our trust in a wholly different paradigm that is, as yet, far from proven by our own experience. Never mind the fact that, intellectually, it seems ridiculously far-fetched anyway. It is not surprising, therefore, that when the chips are down, we fall back on the safe and the familiar and revert to the old way of thinking. Let's face it, our trust in the idea of there being an abundant universe is very fragile and, as we saw at the end of the previous chapter, giving up our attachment to having it be a certain way is almost beyond our capability.

Jerry Stocking is a spiritual teacher and author who wrote a book called *How to Win By Quitting.* In this book he asserts that if you are in the wrong job and you are not happy, then quit. But his essential message is 'quit before you have anything else to go to.' His idea is that if you go looking for a new job before you quit, you are not giving life (Spirit) the opportunity to bestow upon you what you do not have the imagination to create. The idea is to let Spirit find you your ideal work. In other words, give up any attachment to how it might show up and give up the need to control your life. That requires a tremendous leap of faith, trust and a lot of spiritual courage.

Faced with this kind of challenge, the following are examples of the kind of things we do to revert to safety and the familiarity of the old paradigm, and in so doing sabotage the possibility of our manifesting anything.

a) Minimize Expectations
In this way I hedge my bets. If I keep a low expectation about the likelihood of what I have asked for turning up, then I minimize my disappointment and won't feel embarrassed about it not happening. This is often confused with being non-attached but it quite different. It is more akin

to being resigned and or being halfhearted in our intent, which are attributes that repel rather than attract what we ask for. Simply resigning ourselves to the possibility of not having it is a real intention killer.

b) Lose Patience and Take Back Control

Because of our lack of trust we have a tendency to have a very short "surrender-timespan." If we don't get what we want within the time frame we envisioned when setting the intention, we have a tendency to assume that the Universe wasn't listening, didn't hear it correctly or has made a mistake. The worst-case scenario is that we take back control and assume the responsibility for making it happen. But even if we don't do that, just having that doubt can put a kink in the process. Surrender is surrender. There's no going back on it.

c) Create Fear-based, 'What if' Scenarios

"What if I give up my job and nothing turns up?" "What if I get something I don't like?" "What if, through non-attachment, I lose my will and become lazy and apathetic about life?" "What if I miss the signs?"

All these "what-if" stories are grounded in the fear of losing control, which is a big issue for a lot of people. They equate non-attachment with losing control. The fact is, of course, they were never consciously in control in the first place. Their Higher Selves always were the ones orchestrating things. The point is that when we get out of the way and let our Higher Self get on with the job, everything works a whole lot better.

Abraham-Hicks, in their book, *Ask and It Is Given: Learning to Manifest Your Desires,* recommends a very useful device to use on an everyday basis to help you develop the right attitude with regard to this issue. They call it *The Place Mat,* but essentially, it is a To-Do List.

However, it is unusual in the sense that it is divided into two parts vertically. On one side is what you want God to do and on the other is what you need to do. You give God (or your Higher Self), all the big important jobs to do while you just take care of what is in front of you.

TO DO LIST

Me To Do	God To Do
1. Take out the garbage	
2. List what I want in a business partner.	1. Find me my ideal business partner.
3. Read and reply to e-mails	2. Make just the right connections for me that I might be of service to others
4. Plan my Board Meeting coming up tomorrow which might be contentious.	4. Handle the important details of the Board meeting so that the highest and best for everyone is the outcome.

This way, you get to do what needs to be done in worldly, everyday human terms, but you do it all in the knowledge that the really important details are being handled by the

Universe. Your part is small in comparison, but insofar as you have handed so much of what is important and unknowable over to your Higher Self, your contribution to the possibility of a good outcome will be enormous — many times bigger than if you had tried to handle it all yourself. In this sense, your true power is in direct proportion to your willingness to give over control to the Universe and trust the process.

d) Lower Your Vibration

When your vibration is high, you have the power to pull from the implicate order, at will, anything you want. When your energy field is polluted by toxic patterns that lower your vibration, it is much more difficult, if not impossible, to do the same. Here are some ways that you might subconsciously use to lower your vibration in order to sabotage yourself.

i. Talking to the Wrong People

If you share your dreams with skeptics and people who are still committed to the old paradigm, don't be surprised if your dreams don't manifest. Their disbelief is contagious. Even if they don't actually say anything negative, their energy will do serious damage to your intentionality.

Even your best friends have the potential to be your worst enemies in this regard. I learned this in the early 1990's when I was really struggling financially. At the time I was hanging out with some great people who, like me, were interested in the idea of creating one's own reality, but they were just as stuck as I was as far as prosperity was concerned.

One day it occurred to us that we might be supporting each other in staying stuck. In observing ourselves closely, we noticed that if any one of us seemed to be moving forward, we would feel a twinge of jealousy or envy. Then a thought would arise — "If he gets ahead, that means I am left behind and alone in my lack of success." Even though we would say we were pleased for them and in support of their progress, our energy indicated otherwise. What we really wanted was everyone in the group to stay exactly where they were so we could endlessly commiserate with each other about our bad luck. We became experts at this.

Our solution, finally, was for the whole group to go up to the mountains for a weekend retreat. The intent was to find a way to break through the fears and issues that caused us to want to stay small. The first day and a half was very difficult and there was a lot of unpleasantness until someone finally got real and began sharing from their heart. That opened it up for everyone to surrender and let go. After this retreat, everyone in the group began to manifest great opportunities and to move forward in their lives. The group sabotage was finally over.

ii. Denying Your Feelings
In the story above, the breakthrough came at two important points. The first was when we became aware

of our authentic feelings of jealousy, envy and fear that arose when any one of us appeared to be generating success. The second came when we began to share those feelings and explored what was underlying them.

Follow your feelings. They give you excellent feedback and will lead you to discover the core-negative beliefs that would otherwise limit you, such as "I don't deserve prosperity," or "I'm not worthy," and so on.

iii. Denying Your Doubt

The biggest impediment to manifesting your dreams is your own doubt. However, in order to overcome doubt we must first recognize it, accept it and be present to it. Only then can we release it. The antidote to doubt is the experience of success, even if it only comes in small incremental steps. (See next chapter.)

iv. Holding onto the Past

Nothing lowers your vibration more than refusing to let go of your victim story about things that have happened in the past about which you have resentment, regret, disappointment, anger, sadness, grief and so on. It is one of the main tenets of this book, and the *Radical Empowerment* program, that *Radical Forgiveness* must come first. That means totally transforming your victim story by being willing to recognize the perfection in what happened and realizing that there is nothing to forgive.

Chapter 11
Training Wheels

Once you have mastered a skill to the point where it becomes second nature to you, unlearning it in order to replace it with another becomes a real challenge. Through centuries of training, we have become masterful in the art of "getting by" and have become extremely well-practiced and skilled in the art of creating lack and limitation.

Replacing this skill with the art of manifesting abundance is clearly not going to be a breeze. It is a skill that needs to be learned, and since most of us are coming from being steeped in the old paradigm of shortage and limitation, the learning curve is going to be steep. Therefore, in order to become proficient in the art of manifestation, we need to apply to the task what we already know about the nature of skill and skill acquisition.

Every skill set has its cognitive component, and *Radical Manifestation* is no exception. We need to become aware of this knowledge since, in order to be successful, we are required not only to reject one paradigm for another, but to change the habits of a lifetime. It is very important, therefore, that we study the basics of *Radical Forgiveness* first since this gives the metaphysical framework of both *Radical Empowerment* and *Radical Manifestation.*

In addition to its knowledge base, a skill is, by definition, a highly complex set of operations that, once mastered, becomes a singularity in movement and execution. To acquire such an expertise one must practice each part of the skill separately before combining them into the one operation. This means breaking the skill down into discrete and simple steps and then practicing putting it all together under conditions that are conducive to learning with minimal risk of failure.

The basic elements of the skill involved in *Radical Manifestation* have already been outlined in the previous chapters. These are: getting clear about what you want, stating why you want it, visualizing yourself already having it, affirming that you have it now, feeling the gratitude, moving your baseline intention up to the next level, handing it over to Spirit, and letting go of the attachment.

Given the extent of our skepticism and doubt, we would be stretching our proficiency in the art of manifesting beyond its elastic limit if we tried to apply all these disparate operations to something way outside of our experience.

For example, suppose we currently live in a trailer on the wrong side of the tracks in some "hick" town and we try to manifest something like a luxury mansion close to the beach on some exotic island somewhere. It's not going to happen. It would be the equivalent of reading a book on how to fly a glider and then getting into the seat of a Boeing 747 and assuming that you could fly it right away.

Baby Steps
The answer is to develop the skill slowly by taking baby steps and to practice frequently on things that don't matter. I recommend you set a simple and inconsequential intention every day as soon as you get out of bed. Then, just before going to bed simply review the extent to which you attracted that into your experience. Make this a habit.

For example, at the beginning, you could set an intention to have a lot of people smile at you today, or say something of an appreciative nature to you. Notice when they do and then as you review your day, make a note in your journal about the ones you particularly remember.

Pick some things you have a liking for or personal affinity to, and form the intention to manifest them in some way in your life on a particular day and see if it happens or not. Suppose, for example, you have a particular liking for squirrels. Make an intention that at least one will appear in close proximity to you today. Use all the disparate skills you know to give energy to your intention and see if the squirrel turns up. If more than one appears, so much the better. Note it in your journal and give yourself credit for having created the squirrel. Do not write it off as mere chance or coincidence. That's just another way to sabotage yourself.

Incremental Success

When you are learning a new skill, ensuring incremental success at each stage is important in order to build confidence and belief. So be sure to form intentions in the early stage that actually have a fairly high probability of being responded to. The squirrel intention, for instance, would be a good choice if you happen to walk through a park on your way to work. Your ability to project attraction would not need to be extremely strong for it to produce a squirrel under those circumstances. If on the other hand, your entire journey to work was done on the subway, it would require a massive amount of attraction power to produce a squirrel on a subway train. Setting impossible intentions and goals is a common way to sabotage ourselves.

Creating Parking Spaces

In the 80s and 90s, when people first began experimenting with the idea that we create our own reality, the "sport of the day" became creating a parking space just where and when we needed one. People would boast to their friends about how they could always create a parking space. Never mind that the rest of their lives were in turmoil and out of control — they at least could produce a parking space!

Well, even if it does seem a little passé now, why not take up that challenge again, assuming, that is, you live in a place where parking is at a premium and difficult to find under most circumstances. Just see how many times you can produce the perfect parking spot just when you need it. If that is not applicable to you, think of something else of that nature that would work for you.

Increase the Challenge Gradually

As your rate of success in manifesting smiles, squirrels, parking spaces and whatever else you choose to manifest each day increases, you can raise the level of difficulty a couple of notches. However, you should still create intentions that are quite likely to result in success and are relatively inconsequential. It is too early to put pressure on yourself.

You probably need to keep working at this level for several months so you develop your confidence on a solid foundation of experience. Keep the daily journal going to record your increasing skill and ability. As you feel your confidence increasing and your doubt receding, then increase the challenge still more.

Then you can begin to work on more serious and meaningful intentions; ones that require a lot more work on your part to create the energy of attraction and in which you have some emotional investment. At that point you will have really begun to put it all together and be on your way to being able to demonstrate mastery in *Radical Manifestation.*

Chapter 12
Drawing Spirit a Picture

As we have already said in earlier chapters, most of the work with *Radical Manifestation* is a matter of getting out of the way. To be even more precise, this means getting the rational mind out of the way so our spiritual intelligence can engage with Universal Intelligence in the Divine dance of creation.

One of the most time-honored ways of doing this is to construct a visual message that is symbolic of the things that we want to attract to us. Pictures, mandalas, sketches, collages and the like tend to allow us to bypass the rational mind while engaging other parts of our psyche that are connected to our spiritual intelligence.

Treasure Mapping
Again, harking back to the 80s and 90s, the most common form of this was a process known as treasure mapping. This involved combing through a pile of magazines and

cutting out pictures and graphic symbols that struck us as meaningful in terms of what we wanted to create in our lives. The idea then was to glue these items onto a large posterboard in order to make an attractive collage which we would store in our home somewhere as a visual reminder of our dreams.

Another way was simply to use crayons, markers and other drawing instruments to construct the picture depicting all the things we wanted to create. The important thing was to make it colorful and attractive.

Once completed, the tendency was to more or less forget them, or at least not look at them much for quite some months. But when one did look at them it was quite surprising to see the extent to which the dreams enfolded into the collage or picture had actually come to fruition.

While at the time one might have simply assumed that they had come about through the ordinary circumstances of life as we know it, seeing them on the treasure map as our original intentions reminded us that not so long ago they were just ideas in our consciousness. That then forced us to wonder if indeed we had actually drawn it to ourselves through the law of attraction.

Several years ago, JoAnn and I envisaged ourselves buying some land and building a home on it that would be in two parts. One pod would be our personal living quarters while the other would house our offices, studio and workshop space. We made just a small outline sketch of this idea in one corner of the paper on which we had crammed a whole lot of other stuff, and then hung it on the back of our bedroom door. Nothing ever came of it; it was one of those ideas that just got forgotten — or so it seemed. Only quite recently did we look again at the drawing and realize that the idea had in fact manifested.

The way it had come about was that last year we bought some television equipment in order to make DVDs for training purposes. However, there was no space left in our own home for a recording studio so we asked the Universe for a solution. Well, it just so happened that the house next door to us become available for rent right at that moment. Also, at that same time, Dana, who had agreed to come on board to assist me in getting our corporate program launched, needed a home since she was moving from Phoenix to Atlanta to be part of the company. The house next door was the perfect solution for both of us. She moved in and created a home office while we rented one of the rooms from her for our studio and stored much of our inventory in the garage. Although it is not exactly what we had envisioned, it was close enough in concept to be almost uncanny and it has served our purpose admirably.

Our prayers had indeed been answered, but that fact almost escaped our notice because it wasn't answered in precisely the form we had envisioned it. But the truth was that we had attracted the perfect solution without having to move or spend an enormous amount of energy, time and money building a new home. Thank you God!

PART FOUR

Manifesting Money

RADICAL MANIFESTATION

Chapter 13
Money Mindfulness

L et me invite you to participate in an experiment —
an experiential test of "mindfulness."

Mindfulness is your ability to observe your own thoughts
as they flit rapidly through your mind. Thoughts can also
evoke feelings, so mindfulness is also about becoming
aware of what happens in one's body in response to a
thought that passes through your mind.

Are you in? Good.

Then turn the page over *NOW!*

Money is

(Fill in the Blank)

What word(s) or phrases instantly came to mind with which to fill in the blank?

_____

_____

_____

Which ones did you think of first?

_____

_____

_____

Which ones did you censure and decide against entering?

_____

_____

_____

What thoughts went through your mind?

_____

_____

_____

_____

_____

Did each thought conflict with the one before it? If so, in what ways did they conflict?

_____

_____

_____

What feelings arose in your body?

_____

Where in your body did you feel them?

_____

Put your hand on the place in your body where the
feelings were most located.

**Now, before you have time to think about it, say out
loud the word "money" — NOW.**

Did you hear how you said it? The tone? The inflection?

Pause for three seconds, and say it again.

Pause for three seconds, and say it again.

Pause for three seconds, and say it again.

Pause for three seconds, and say it again.

You've said the word money now five times. Do your best
to review, in audio memory, how you said the word money
on each occasion.

Are you noticing any difference between each of them?

_____

_____

_____

What did you hear in HOW you said it?

_____

_____

_____

What meaning came through with each attempt?

_____

_____

_____

What feelings arose on each occasion?

_____

_____

_____

How are you feeling now? _____
Have the feelings moved to another part of your body?

What have you learned about how you feel about money?
(Take a few moments to jot down a few things that you've
learned before going on.)

Notes:

_____

_____

_____

_____

_____

_____

_____

Notes:

This is the end of this particular exercise but I invite you to keep observing your thoughts and feelings as you read the following pages. Mindfulness is the first step in deprogramming negative thoughts, ideas and beliefs about money from your subconscious mind, while at the same time strengthening the positive ones.

Chapter 14
Snakes, Sharks & Money

There are very few people in the entire world who do not have extremely strong emotional reactions to snakes. A tiny minority of people love them, but the vast majority have a morbid fear of them and hate them with a vengeance. I am one of them.

Yet the number of deaths per year attributed to snake bites is minuscule compared to, for instance, deaths caused by car accidents. Very few snakes are naturally aggressive and most do their best to avoid contact with human beings and only bite in self-defense.

We have a similar reaction to sharks. Even when we see it on a television screen, there is something about the image of a Great White gliding through the water that makes us shudder. We almost universally identify this creature as the epitome of evil, evoking in most people tremendous fear and hatred.

Yet the facts are that less than a handful of people are killed by sharks in any given year and attacks by sharks are very rare indeed. Even with those that do occur, the evidence is very strong that attacks are a result of a person on a surf board looking a lot like a seal when viewed from underneath. Most attacks are therefore an 'innocent' mistake on the part of the shark.

Irrational Fear

Clearly, our emotional responses to these creatures are completely irrational and unfounded, totally unwarranted and out of all proportion to the (infinitesimal) threat that they pose. Why we have this deep universal fear of snakes when most of us will never be confronted with one is not fully understood, but it is certainly visceral, archetypal and real. On the other hand, our fear of sharks is more likely due to films and media-hyped stories than anything else.

Emotional Reactions to Money

Money evokes at least as many, if not more, irrational emotional responses as do sharks and snakes — and with no less intensity. In the same way as we hate snakes and fear sharks, we relate to money with the same (though disguised) kind of dread. We think we love it, but the exact opposite is the case. It universally evokes fear. Subconsciously, we avoid it to the same degree as we do the most poisonous of snakes and the most aggressive of sharks.

[It is interesting to note that we describe people who try to sell us things as "snake-oil" salesmen and those who want to lend us money at high interest rates as "loan sharks." Also, in situations where large amounts of money move competitively between people, we refer to that as "a shark environment."]

Affluent People

You might ask, what about the folks who appear to be really quite well off? Do they hate money?

Possibly so because, in America anyway, most of them are mortgaged up to the hilt, carry huge credit card debt and have their lives organized in such a way that if their circumstances were to change, like losing their job, or a business going belly up, they too would find themselves in trouble. They hate money because it can be withdrawn from them at any moment and bring down their house of cards. They spend fortunes on insurance and lawyers, and hate both.

On the Edge

Affluent people live life like the surfers live it, but unlike the fish sharks, the money sharks really are dangerous to your health. Ask anyone who has been unable to meet their obligation to pay off their credit card debt! At least if a fish shark takes a bite at you, it usually spits you out once it realizes you are not a seal! Credit card companies will gnaw you to death.

The Wealthy

Even some of the wealthiest of people who appear to be financially secure in every way seem terrified of losing their money and act as if they never have enough of it. They hate money because it owns them and consumes them. [The ones who seem to enjoy it the most are those that love to give much of it away for no other reason than for the pure joy of giving. Such people are rare. Most rich people give it away only to save on taxes, to get what they want or to influence others.]

People Who "Love" Money
This is really a term we reserve for people who are *obsessed* with money. They think that money has intrinsic value and they believe (erroneously) that the more of it they have the better they will feel. They don't. Ebenezer Scrooge loved money until he saw what it did to him and those around him; and look what happened to Midas!

Living With Snakes and Sharks
In places like Africa and Australia where there are many snakes, the people who live there find ways to live with them. They regard them as part of the natural order and tolerate them as such. Surfers make a calculated assessment and, because they enjoy surfing so much, go into the water to do it anyway, in spite of the risk that they might get mistaken for a seal.

A Necessary Evil
In much the same way, we tolerate the idea that we need money, even though we hate it. Some people even refer to it as a necessary evil and see it as the root of all evil.

In order to be right about our belief in shortage and to therefore protect ourselves from being overwhelmed by abundance, the vast majority of us make sure that we have only just enough to get by on, week by week, month by month, year by year, and very little more.

[Note: I am not really talking about societies where extreme poverty is so endemic that virtually no money is in circulation and that virtually everyone is simply one small step above starvation level. I'm talking about economies where money flows relatively freely.]

This is a shocking statement to make, but it is true nevertheless. What we perceive as enough to get by on can vary considerably, but the fact remains that we are masters of the game of making sure that we have only just enough to meet our basic needs. If there is any left over, we squander it as fast as possible.

Homeless

In spite of the fact that on any given day vast sums of money are moving around the globe every second and that money is multiplying all the time, most people manage to attract no more than just enough of it to keep from being homeless. And yet only a tiny fraction of people actually become homeless. Why is this?

If we believe, as most people do, that the amount of money we have depends on a whole bunch of circumstances that are essentially outside of our control, how is it that circumstances don't push more people into homelessness when the line between mere getting by and being home-less is so fine? And it is extremely fine when you consider how large the range of possibility or "buffer" actually is.

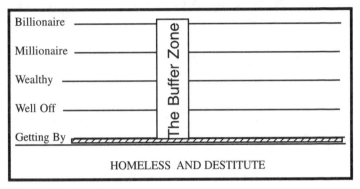

Fig. 10: The Buffer Zone

If it were actually true that outside economic circumstances were the only factors determining at what level we play on that scale, and given that we have that whole arena to play in, from merely getting by to being a billionaire, doesn't it look weird that we can actually spend all our lifetime in that tiny space between the "getting by" line and the des-titute line _⚹⚹⚹⚹⚹⚹⚹⚹_ without going under?

Wouldn't you think that, given the small degree of error required to tip us under that line, or over it for that matter, we would be in and out of homelessness on a fairly regular basis if all it depended on was chance and the vagaries of macroeconomics? By its very nature, a market-based sys-tem is so dynamic and forever in a state of flux that we as "the basic unit of economic activity" would be bouncing in and out of homelessness like yo-yos if that was all there was to it.

124

Fine Tuning

Don't you think there might be some other factor involved that is capable of fine tuning our individual financial situation much more accurately and subtly than the crude, macroeconomic factors of the economy? Of course there is, and you know only too well that it's us: you and me and all the others who have bought into the myths around money. We fine tune the system with our consciousness.

We have actually made an art form out of the process of limiting our supply of money so that it fits just nicely into that narrow band that keeps us in our comfort zone — mere survival mode. We are experts at it. We can take ourselves right to the very edge and yet, at the last moment, manifest just enough to save our butts. If we find ourselves receiving much more that this, we find ways to lose it, and fast. Even if we win the lottery, we'll find a way to get back to where we are comfortable.

No Surprise

The ideas that the vast majority of people have a subconscious "aversion to money" should come as no surprise to the readers, especially if they have read all the preceding chapters of this book. We know without a shadow of a doubt that we create our world according to our beliefs, attitudes, values and assumptions, so why should it be any different when it comes to money? Where our thoughts go, so energy goes.

Our minds are stacked out with limiting beliefs about money and our relationship to it. Those beliefs, along with the

125

emotions that fuel them, determine where each one of us will play in the money game and how well we will do. It's the law.

Law of Attraction
Our beliefs and attitudes have a certain vibration and, according the Law of Attraction, will attract to themselves only those things which match that vibration. We all know that the dominant belief around money is that there is a shortage of it. (My father used to say, "Money doesn't grow on trees, you know!") We also know that like attracts like, so it is mandated that a belief in shortage will attract shortage. It's that simple.

Go back and look at the notes you made on the page subsequent to your mindfulness exercise. Even if you didn't actually get in touch with any of your negative money beliefs, it's highly likely that you noticed something in your voice that indicated that you have some that are not conducive to financial prosperity. Then there was that feeling in your gut when you said the word "money." What do you think that might mean?

Law of Association
This law says that if you have a fear of A, and A is the same as B, by association you will automatically be scared of B. Given that you have a fear of sharks and you associate having a lot of money, or making money, with sharks, guess what?

126

What other associations have you paired in with money? Fear of success maybe? Fear of being like someone you know, perhaps? Power to corrupt? Need to struggle?

Make an Inventory

This might be a good moment to do an inventory of possible negative associations that you have with money. What did your parents and family members teach you about money? How did they behave towards money, and what thoughts did they have around money that might have found their way into your consciousness?

It would definitely be helpful to spend time on this exercise so you can establish what your internal money program actually is. Don't skimp time on this. It could be very revealing.

Who Taught You?

When you have completed this inventory, make a list of the people responsible for teaching you those beliefs that have kept you less that abundant moneywise?

1. _____
2. _____
3. _____
4. _____
5. _____
6. _____

Then proceed to do at least one Radical Forgiveness Worksheet on each one of them.

127

Use either the hard copy paper ones (downloadable from *www.radicalforgiveness.com*) or go to this same web site and use the interactive, on-line Worksheet Tutorial version.

It is essential that you do this, for as long as you hold those people responsible for teaching you these ideas, the more liable you will be to subconsciously lay the blame at their feet for you not being abundant. That disempowers you because you subconsciously put the cause for your lack of abundance "out there" instead of "in here." Once you have done that, you have given your power over to them and thereafter you will remain unable to create what you want. You will be stuck.

Doing the *Radical Forgiveness* worksheets on each one of them will dissolve the energy surrounding each of the beliefs that they taught you. It is one of the quickest ways I know of changing your core-negative beliefs.

Chapter 15
The Meaning of Money

From what we have observed in the previous chapter, it might look as though the number of people in the world who relate to money with happiness and joy, *no matter how much or how little they have,* are about as numerous as those who love snakes. Those few who do relate to money with happiness and joy seem to have the following characteristics.

• A complete disregard for money as an end in itself.
• A love of the freedom money gives them to make choices.
• A seemingly natural ability to attract the money they need.
• A heightened state of openness to receive money.
• A high need to share it abundantly with others.
• A desire to make it work for the common good.
• A firm belief in the natural abundance of the Universe.
• An unshakable trust that their needs will always be met.
• A complete absence of any attachment to having money knowing that it will always manifest when needed.

As you would imagine, these people are quite rare. That's because they would need to be people who are living their life totally from a belief in the new paradigm to the total exclusion of the old one. And there aren't many of those around. If you look again at that list, you will see that each one of the characteristics would depend upon the person's consciousness being grounded in the new paradigm. Let's examine each one of these in more detail.

• **A complete disregard for money as an end itself.**
This person realizes that money has no inherent value beyond the meaning people give it. The meanings people attach to money are all related to the old paradigm to which this person doesn't subscribe. For example: money means security; money equals power; money connotes success; and so on. This person is not willing to invest money with the power to define him/her nor to run his/her life.

• **A love of the freedom money gives them to make choices.**
This is the only meaning they are willing to give money. For as long as they have some, it does give them freedom to make choices, even if the range is limited. The more money one has, the more choices one can make about how one lives. However, this person realizes that it is the choices that one makes that determines happiness, not the amount of money one has.

- **A seemingly natural ability to attract money**

  You've met people like this, I know. They are money magnets. Money just flows to them. However, not all of them are people you would automatically associate with the new paradigm. The kind of people I am thinking about would be the ones who easily attract money to themselves but who also satisfy the other criteria. Most would not.

- **A heightened state of openness to receive money.**

  What was said in the previous paragraph could easily apply to this one, but what I mean here is the kind of allowing that comes from knowing that money has no meaning, that it is neutral and has no power in and of itself. It is devoid of any issues of deservability, responsibility, worthiness to receive or fear. It is a state of pure openness to receive or not to receive.

- **A high need to share it abundantly with others.**

  This kind of person feels no need to hold onto money and gets a real kick out of giving it away in good measure. This is different from the kind of tithing where people give in the expectation of getting more back than they gave, or where they gave to get a tax-break. It is giving out of the sheer joy of giving knowing that there's plenty more in the spiritual pipeline.

- **A desire to make it work for the common good.**

  This person understands the idea of money being energy and the difference it can make when directed in ways that serve humanity, the planet, the animal kingdom and all of life.

131

- **A firm belief in the abundance of the universe.**

  The is the baseline idea and it is non-negotiable. Without this one idea as the anchor, none of the others would have meaning. They all reference this one idea. It is the core belief within the new paradigm. Without this, it is nothing.

- **An unshakable trust that their needs will always be met.**

  This arises out of the solid belief that abundance is the natural condition of the Universe and indicates a willingness to put that to the test at any time.

- **A complete absence of any attachment to having money knowing that it will manifest when needed — and it always does.**

  This is the person who is truly free; free from the need to have more money than he/she needs and is totally at peace in the knowledge that whether money arrives or not, all is well.

Of these nine characteristics, the first six could be applied to people operating in either paradigm or straddling both at the same time. The last three, however, have no such flexibility in their definition. They are as fundamental to the new paradigm as they are poison to the old one.

Doubt Persists

As we have discussed earlier, there are very few people who are, in evolutionary terms, operating wholly from the new paradigm of total abundance. The reason for that is that we are still at stage two in the process of shifting from the old to the new, which means we are straddling the two. With one foot in each, we would really like to embrace the idea of limitless abundance, but we still doubt its possibility given our everyday experience of shortage and limitation.

A Model

The only person I know of who was fully able to demonstrate the principles of abundance in his life was Buckminster Fuller. Bucky was definitely someone who was totally grounded in the new paradigm. He was in fact one of those who began to articulate it when it was really new to most of us, way back in the 50s and 60s.

Apparently he made it a practice to zero his bank account at the end of every month. Whatever he had at the end of the month, he would give it away. He drove his accountants mad, but he was a scientist who understood energy and he regarded money as nothing more than that. He also knew that for it to be useful, it needs to flow. So he kept it moving.

For him, it was like breathing. You breathe it in; then you breathe it out. No effort at all. On the other hand, if you hold your breath for too long, you die.

Feedback

Nothing will act more clearly as a barometer of our belief in, or our commitment to, either the old or the new paradigm than how we relate to and behave with money. The

133

extent to which we can really trust the Universe and let go of our money issues will show us exactly where we are in the process of shifting from one to the other. Not only will we get frequent opportunities to observe this from within, but, since money is moving all the time in our lives, it will give us constant feedback, in very concrete terms, about where we are at any one time.

Shift Happens With Money

If you want to speed up the paradigm shift in yourself, there is no better way to do it, in my opinion, than to play with money. Not that you have to do it like Bucky, I hasten to add. Even though you will need to move out of your comfort zone to some degree, there's no point in stressing yourself out so much that you blow your circuits and crash-land right back into the old paradigm. There's no reason why we can't learn to ride this thing with training wheels along the lines I have suggested in previous chapters.

Chapter 16
An Energy Game

First, let's get clear about the nature of the game that we are playing here with *Radical Manifestation.* It's an energy game; identical to the one that became the basis for *Radical Forgiveness* even before I understood what it was and how it worked.

I eventually came to understand that the key to instantaneous relief from the tyranny of the past was not in trying to change anything at the level of physical reality, nor even at the level of mind. Rather it was in dissolving the "energy complex" that was attached to a painful experience.

I discovered that the energy complex, which existed as an energy block in one's physical and subtle bodies, dissolved simply as a result of the person making a request to their spiritual intelligence that it be handled automatically at the spiritual level — and it was. He or she made that request by using one of the *Radical Forgiveness* tools.

There was nothing else one needed to do and there was no requirement that the person have any belief in the concept of *Radical Forgiveness* for it to work. All that was required was a "willing skepticism;" a willingness to entertain the possibility that what happened was part of a Divine plan and happened for a reason. All that was left to do then was to be willing to go through the process using one of the tools.

Transformation
What this proves to me is that working hard to change or reprogram the subconscious ideas, thoughts, beliefs, assumptions and emotions attached to the original event that couldn't be forgiven is not necessary. All one has to do is to find a way to collapse the energy field that contains them all. That process is simply a matter of turning it over to our spiritual intelligence.

This transforms the situation since we begin to operate out of the new paradigm immediately, even if only in relation to that specific event. It is the only paradigm that our spiritual intelligence understands and operates from. This means that almost immediately the assumptions of that paradigm become truly meaningful to that situation while the assumptions of the old paradigm fall away. Blame gives way to gratitude; enemies become healing angels; love replaces fear and so on. That's transformation.

If it works for "energy complexes" like unforgiveness, which is universally understood to be very resistant to change, then there is no reason why this approach won't work with other energy complexes, like lack of abundance.

When you examine a *Radical Forgiveness* worksheet, it has all the assumptions of *Radical Forgiveness* imbedded in the questions it poses. So, as explained in Chapter 6, the worksheet serves as a "fake-it-til-you-make-it," bridge that helps to move us from one paradigm to the other.

So why not have the same thing for money and abundance? It will work in exactly the same way, serving as the same kind of bridge as before, supporting you in faking your belief in the notion of an infinitely abundant Universe even while you doubt it.

So, in the *Radical Empowerment Kit,* I have included, in addition to a general manifestation worksheet, another one specific to money. It is entitled the *Money Consciousness Worksheet.*

This is a way of employing your spiritual intelligence in the process of actually creating an abundance consciousness. Giving it over to this powerful part of who you are frees you from the need to spend a fortune going to seminars that focus on reprogramming your mind about money. We simply let sleeping dogs lie, ignore the mind and, through the worksheet, ask Spirit to take care of it.

In the following chapter we list some of the assumptions about money that are in accordance with the new paradigm so that they become imbedded in your consciousness.

Chapter 17
Assumptions About Money

• **Money is an abstraction and has no inherent value.**
When gold coins were the means of exchange, there was
some inherent value to the coin itself. These days, money
is mostly a series of ones and zeros in a computer program activated by credit and debit cards. It only has value
when it is exchanged for something and then it ceases to
be money anyway.

• **Money is energy.**
Money is energy, and as such it is as much subject to the
law of attraction as any other sort of energy. It will flow
towards those who are the most willing to receive it, have
a use for it, and have no problem asking for it.

• **Money is neutral.**
Money will flow to whomever attracts it, whether it be a
hardened criminal or a devout priest. It doesn't care. It
will flow to people doing spiritual work too, so long as

those people don't block it with silly ideas like spiritual people shouldn't earn money doing spiritual work.

It is untrue that doing what you love means that money will automatically follow. It will only do so if you are a magnet for it. Then it will. You cannot simply assume money will flow to you. You have to attract it while at the same time be unattached to having it: a delicate balancing act.

• There is no shortage of money.

Since money is energy and energy is limitless, money is also limitless. Right now there's more of the stuff in circulation than you could ever imagine. And they keep printing more of it. The more people there are on the planet, the more money there is. It keeps multiplying. There is as much money in the system as the system demands. The more we give it away, the more it expands.

Money is love.

Love is all there is. It is the energy that runs the Universe. Money is also energy, so money and love can be synonymous. Love makes the world go around. Money does the same. Love expands the heart, while money gives us the opportunity to experience heartfelt feelings like gratitude, generosity, compassion and love itself. Like attracts like, so love attracts money because they are the same. Greed, envy and lust will generate money too, but it will be accompanied by fear, not love. Which would you rather have?

• **Abundance is the natural condition of the universe.**
The idea of infinite abundance is fundamental to money
consciousness even though most of our abundance comes
to us free. Money is not needed for such things as sun-
shine, rain, a smile, a cheerful word, a touch, a kiss, a
birdsong, the smell of a flower and so on and so on. Actually, when you begin to think about it, only a very small
amount of what we really love about life comes about as a
consequence of having money. Once you have your food,
and a warm comfortable place to live in, the rest is relative
and most of it is free.

• **Money has no power.**
When we become aware of the power that we have to
create the circumstances of our lives, we realize that we
are no more at the mercy of money than we are of any
outer circumstance. The real source of our power lies
within, and that is our own spiritual intelligence and its
power to connect to Source. There is not a single person
on this planet who is denied access to that. We are all
equally powerful in that regard, no matter how much money
we have.

• **Money is our teacher.**
As spiritual beings having a human experience, we are
blessed with the ability to experience life and access our
power through our feelings. Money provides many opportunities to feel our feelings and, through those experiences, to grow and learn.

PART 5

Weight Loss

RADICAL MANIFESTATION

Chapter 18
Body Mindfulness

As we discussed at the beginning of Part Four, it is helpful to develop mindfulness about things in our lives that we give our power away to or allow to control us. In Part Four it was money. This chapter is devoted to the body and the issue of weight in particular.

The ability to observe your own thoughts as they relate to your body while they pass almost imperceptably through your mind is what we mean by "body mindfulness." Let's try a similar experiment on this like we did on money mindfulness.

Turn the page *NOW!*

I

_____

(Fill in the blank)

My Body

What word or words came to mind the instant you looked at the open sentence and saw that you had to fill in the blank?

I **love** my body,

I **hate** my body,

I **respect** my body,

I **care for** my body,

I **loathe** my body,

I **reject** my body,

I **accept** my body,

What feelings arose as you mentally filled in the blank?

disgust
shame
love
guilt
sadness
frustration
anger
warmth
other _____

My Body Is

_____

(Fill in the blank)

What words came to mind to fill in that blank?

> Beautiful
> Ugly
> Shameful
> Too Fat
> Too Thin
> OK/Not OK
> Unhealthy
> Healthy
> Supportive
> Awesome
> Fit/Unfit
> Lovely
> Sick
> Others _____

What feelings did you notice arising in you as you mentally filled in the blank?

> disgust
> shame
> love
> guilt
> sadness
> frustration
> anger
> warmth
> other _____

I Am
<u>NOT</u>
My Body

What thoughts went through your mind when you saw that statement?

> But I <u>AM</u> my body.
> What a relief to realize that!
> I am free to be me!
> I need no longer identify with my body.
> My body's pain is not my pain.
> My body is sick but I am not.
> If I am not my body, who am I?
> If I am not my body, what am I?
> I am OK no matter what my body is doing.
> My body is my vehicle for living life.
> I project my negativity onto my body.

What feelings came up for you around this statement?

> Relief
> Disbelief
> Compassion
> Love
> Acceptance
> Gratitude

Chapter 19
Body Awareness

If nothing else, this little exercise probably made you stop and think about how much importance we attach to the body and the degree to which we identify with it. We dress it, trim it, shave it, bathe it, uplift it, perfume it, beautify it, augment it, adorn it, medicate it, exercise it, feed it and in numerous others ways focus an enormous amount of attention upon it. Given the size and value of the fashion industry, you could even say we are obsessed with it. No wonder we become convinced that we are our bodies!

The truth is, of course, is that we existed before we had a body and we will continue to exist after we have experienced our physical death and dropped the body. Just like we rent a car for a specific journey, the body is something we take on and use for the duration of our earth-walk and then discard once the journey is over. It arises out of the earth and returns to the earth.

Why Take on a Body?

Interestingly enough though, in spite of our obsession with the physical body, and as much as we have studied it and come to know its intricate workings, we have all but ignored the most fundamental question of all. Why do we have a body? Why would a spiritual being who is free to move around at will within the World of Divine Existence decide to lower its vibration in order to become encumbered with a body that is dense and heavy and prone to breaking down?

Separation Sucks

I believe the reason that we do it is to be able to experience separation and all that comes with that. And we do it in order that we might develop a deeper awareness of Oneness. It's an important lesson for us spiritual beings to master and it is no easy task, especially since, for much of the incarnation experience we cease to have remembrance of the spiritual world. Separation is experienced as real and painful — and it sucks! That's why we need forgiveness.

"It's the Emotions Stupid!"

The other part of the agreement we made with Spirit was to be willing to have the experience of separation as purely an emotional event. And for that, a body is essential. That's because an emotion is "a thought attached to a feeling." If you don't have a body to provide the feeling element, you have only a thought form. So the primary function of the body is to give us the opportunity to feel our feelings and to have emotions. The human experience, therefore, is meant to be an emotional experience, and the degree to which we won't allow ourselves to have our emotions, or to experience life through our feelings, is the extent to which we are denying our purpose for being here.

So, it is all the more extraordinary that in spite of all our scientific knowledge about how the body works, and our seemingly endless obssesion with it, there has been precious little focus on the "feeling" element. It was not until Candace Pert wrote her book, *Molecules of Emotion,* that anyone really bothered to look at the direct role the body plays in helping us feel our feelings and, by extension, to experience the pain of separation. It has always been assumed that emotion is in the mind and has little to do with the body, but you only have to think about what happens in the body when you have an emotional experience to know that the body is fully involved.

Body Hatred
If the body is our spiritual vehicle for taking us into and through the deep pain of separation, is it any wonder that we are not only obsessed with our bodies, but essentially hate them for precisely that reason?

Even though our memories of existence prior to incarnation are dim at best, or for the most part non-existent, don't you think that part of us might remember what it is like to be just spirit and not encumbered with a body? Isn't it possible that we might have some resentment about having to carry this burden? If so, doesn't it make sense that we might project all our guilt and rage about being separate and in pain onto our body? After all, having taken on a body as a symbol of separation, it follows that the body must also symbolize the intense pain that inevitably accompanies the sense of separation.

Self Hatred

In this world of separation that we have created and live in, one of the ways to stay stuck there is to consistently blame, justify, deny and project the pain of having to endure separation onto something else. We do this in one of two ways. We either project it onto someone or something else "out there," or we turn it back and project it onto our own body. Because we are so identified with our bodies, the hatred we feel towards our bodies becomes generalized as self-hatred.

The Weight Issue

This preamble should serve as a backdrop to the one body issue over which we constantly obsess and which serves as one of the most convenient targets for our self-hatred that I wish now to address. That is the question of weight.

156

Chapter 20
The Weight Issue

According to a 2002 report in the *Journal of the American Medical Association,* approximately two thirds of the adult population in America is overweight. Millions of dollars each year are spent by hundreds of thousands of people trying to lose weight through dieting, exercise, drugs, supplements, hypnosis and other weight control measures. Most of them fail, especially in the long term. They may produce a short-term weight loss, but invariably it comes back on. The only programs that do seem to have a modest degree of success are those that, like Weight Watchers, provide an enormous amount of ongoing community support of a psychological and life-style nature.

The vast majority of programs focus on the physical factors associated with excessive weight gain and virtually ignore or, at best, give only a passing nod to the emotional factors.

My intention in this section, therefore, is to address head-on some of the emotional issues that seem explain why people pack on the weight and adopt life-style patterns that only add to the problem.

Physical and Emotional

In my experience in helping people deal with their emotional issues through *Radical Forgiveness,* I have noticed that a person's emotional issues are frequently reflected in their physical body in some way or another. It can appear as disease, tissue breakdown and so on, but for a great many people, it is reflected in the form of excess weight.

What the ratio is between physical and emotional factors in accounting for weight gain is difficult to say, but I would hazard a guess that most people's weight problems are somewhere in the region of being 75 percent physical and life-style-related in nature and 25 percent emotional. However, this will obviously vary from person to person. I have encountered people who I estimate have that ratio reversed. Even then this is a false distinction, since many of the physical factors themselves have an emotional cause, or at the very least, an emotional component.

The Physical Factors

The physical factors include the things that people are more or less born with, such as body type, metabolism, food aversions, blood type, appetite, genetics and a general predisposition to hold weight.

Life-Style Factors

These include things like exercise, stress, acquired food preferences, addictions, eating habits, substance abuse, over-eating and the like. Peer pressure, cultural norms, mass media influences and even the diet industry itself contribute to the problem with its constant obsession with food fads and life-style fashions.

This is as much as I am going to say about physical and life-style factors in this section, except to say that you can use the *Radical Manifestation* process to create the body you want and the circumstances that would support that. *Radical Empowerment* gives you the tools with which to do this.

Having said that, though, I have already made it clear that in order to be able to manifest anything, our energy field has to be relatively clear and that our vibration needs to be high. Body issues are no exception. If we have emotional issues underlying our weight problem, these have to be cleared out first in order for us to be able to make these kinds of a changes. That means using *Radical Forgiveness* technology before doing the "ideal body" manifestation process.

Again, "It's the Emotions, Stupid!"

It is clear to me that our bodies reflect our emotional health. Many people deal with their emotions by suppressing and repressing their feelings, which is an extremely unhealthy strategy. Repressed emotional baggage can manifest as disease or can literally shows up as physical baggage in the form of excess weight.

159

Functional Fat

No amount of dieting will get rid of excess body fat if it is serving an emotional function. The most common function it performs is protection. This can be protection from generalized hurt and rejection, but most frequently it is used to protect from imagined or real sexual attack.

Protection

The sexual abuse of children by their parents, grandparents, step-parents, mother's boyfriends, siblings, baby-sitters and others is rampant in our society. It is estimated that one in five adults were sexually molested in their childhood years.

The only way a powerless child can deal with this is through the mechanisms of denial, repression and disassociation. However, such attacks leave a powerful energetic imprint on the body, generated and sustained by a potent mixture of repressed fear and guilt. (The guilt arises because they nearly always think of it as their fault). This is frequently made much worse by their own mother's refusing to believe them, if and when they have summoned enough courage to tell. The result is that they simply end up being blamed and punished even more.

The Body Remembers

Even if the mind blocks it out, the cellular structure of the body remembers only too well. So it seeks to protect itself by piling on the fat in those regions previously most affected and thought to be most vulnerable. This not only provides a wall of physical protection against attack, but psychic protection also.

Attractive is Risky

The mind figures that being physically attractive is a risky proposition, so the best way to ward off physical advances is by making oneself decidedly unattractive. What better way to become sexually unattractive than to be obese?

Self-Hatred

The body can also put on excess weight as a way to reinforce feelings of inadequacy and of being unloved. It is like a self-fulfilling prophecy that feeds on itself. The worse I feel about myself, the fatter I become. The fatter I become, the worse I feel about myself. And so it goes, on and on.

It is difficult to know for sure, but I would be willing to hazard a guess that well over half of those who are grossly overweight are that way because they have deeply buried unconscious emotional pain that they are either not aware of or won't deal with.

The Solution

The obvious answer is *Radical Forgiveness.* It is the technology that hundreds of sexual abuse victims and victims of other forms of abuse have used to neutralize and dissolve the energy pattern that kept the guilt, shame and fear frozen in their bodies and surrounded by fat.

The big advantage of the *Radical Forgiveness* approach is that it does not require that the person remember what happened, nor go through the pain of re-enacting the experience. Surprisingly, the *Radical Forgiveness* process is enough.

161

Therapy for the Therapists

It is well known that people in the helping professions tend to choose that line of work in order to focus on helping others deal with their pain rather than deal with their own. Of the many therapists out there who "specialize" in working with sexually abused people, a large proportion of them are themselves abuse "survivors" who have not healed their own pain. Refusing to face it, they keep it totally buried and out of conscious awareness.

The problem with that is that they unconsciously project their own repressed rage onto their clients and encourage them to engage in all sorts of activities that, while they might seem to be healthy things to do, are, in fact, just thinly disguised forms of revenge. The result is that people stay stuck in victimland and do not heal. They continue to see themselves as "victims of abuse," or "abuse survivors," and continue to pack on the functional fat as protection.

It is fashionable, for example, for therapists to strongly suggest that the person confront their abuser and accuse them of their crime. I have yet to see this result in any kind of a healing. It invariably causes a dramatic worsening of the relationship and an increase in the pain for both parties. The thing it does *appear* to do is make the therapist feel better!

With *Radical Forgiveness,* the confront is not necessary. In fact, it is always counterproductive. Much better that the work is done energetically and, initially at least, within the consciousness of the person forgiving. It will then spread out naturally to the others involved. Let me explain.

162

An Energy Experience

The pain that the person feels is in direct proportion to the emotional energy invested, not so much in the event itself, but in the "story" of what happened. (The story is composed of all the thoughts, assumptions, beliefs, feelings, memories and fears connected to the abuse. Most of it is repressed and therefore unconscious.)

That's not to say that the pain isn't real, but what is clear is that the emotional energy invested in the story accounts for a disproportionate amount of the suffering. (Pain is what we experience directly in response to an event. Suffering comes as a result of the thoughts and beliefs we create about the event.)

For example, people who have experienced abuse typically have formed such self-deprecating, wounding beliefs as, *"I am damaged goods; I am no good; I don't deserve respect; I don't count; my needs don't matter; I am flawed; I am dirty; I can't say no; I will never be appreciated for who I am; men will always abuse me,"* and so on. This is what creates the suffering.

The emotional energy invested eventually crystallizes into a highly integrated energy field located in the body. It is this energy field which holds the story in place and keeps the suffering going on.

163

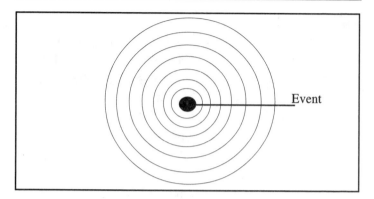

Fig. 11: Energy Field Attached to Event

The way to heal the pain and suffering, therefore, is to simply dissolve that energy field. Once the energy field has collapsed, the story itself loses its power and begins to fade away. There is absolutely no need to go digging up the past, reliving the experience or confronting the abuser.

The dissolution of the energy field occurs through the *Radical Forgiveness* process which comprises the following five stages.

1. Telling the Story
This where the person tells his or her story insofar as he or she knows it consciously. There is no need to try dredging up the unconscious stuff through hypnosis, nor even to prove that it happened. It doesn't matter whether it is true or not, since the objective is not to confront anyone with it, at least not in this process.

[If legal proceedings are necessary, that is a separate issue and nothing I say here has anything to do with

164

what the law might say about the abuse or what might need to be done with the abuser to protect others. This is about forgiveness only, and what happens within the person forgiving. It has nothing to do with the abuser, or anyone else for that matter.]

The important thing in this first stage is to allow the person to express their victim story as only they know it and to have it witnessed and validated — as "their" story.

2. Feeling the Feelings

This usually happens as a consequence of telling the story and is an essential part of the process. It is also the part that most people try to avoid. A common way to avoid it is to intellectualize it, trivialize it, or to "spiritualize" it. We call the latter doing a "spiritual bypass!"

However, it is only through accessing and being willing to fully express the feelings that we have attached to the situation that we can begin the process of dissolving the energy field.

3. Collapse the Energy Field

The energy field begins to collapse when, once having expressed our rage, grief, sadness and hurt, we open our minds and hearts to all the factors relevant to the situation and begin to distinguish what in the story is fact and what is interpretation, what really matters, what is meaningless and what needs are being served by holding onto the story. This is partly rational analysis, but in the context of *Radical Forgiveness* it is but one step in the process of dissolving the energy field and not a "therapy" in and of itself.

4. Reframe the Story
This is the *Radical Forgiveness* step. It is where we open up to the possibility that, if we could see the spiritual big picture (which we cannot), we would become aware that what happened was part of a Divine plan and was intended for our soul's growth. Therefore in that sense nothing wrong happened.

Now, as we know, that is a very difficult idea to accept, and right now the only way we can even work with it is to use a *Radical Forgiveness* worksheet that enables us to say "Yes" to it, even when we don't believe it.

5. Integrate the Story
This involves doing something physical to complete the energetic exchange and to replace, in the physical body at the cellular level, the victim story with the new "perfection" story. This is accomplished by doing the worksheet or using one or more of the other tools. One of the most powerful ways to integrate is to do a (supervised) session of breathwork.

Doing the *Radical Forgiveness* process does more than make the person doing the forgiving feel better. Not only does it collapse the energy field attached to their own personal story, but it begins to collapse the entire energy field surrounding the abuse situation itself, and all those involved, including the abuser. Because they all belong to the same "morphogenetic field,"* (see next page), everyone feels it, and everyone has free will to respond to it in whatever way is best for them spiritually. And it all happens way below the level of awareness.

No one knows that anything is happening, except that they feel different. Something might arise in them that might cause them to feel inclined to say something or do something that might lead to a healing of some sort. Who knows? Our experience is that it happens very frequently — and is far more likely to happen this way than through doing the confrontation.

It also resolves the issue of whether or not the abuse actually happened. Many people have what we call flashbacks or spontaneous recall of early childhood abuse events, and very often there is doubt about the reliability of the recall. For example, it is sometimes thought that a therapist with unresolved abuse issues might be unconsciously transferring their energy to the client. It could also be past-life recall or bleedthrough from the collective unconscious.

When we deal with it through *Radical Forgiveness,* none of this matters. Whatever the origin of the energy field, it is dissolved. The person is free to get on with their lives, no one is accused, falsely or otherwise, and the likelihood of relationships becoming healed are good. Everyone wins.

167

Once this has occurred, the thoughts, feelings and beliefs connecting attractiveness with increased risk of being attacked sexually died at the same time as the energy field dissolved. That means that the reasons for holding weight have also died, so now one is free to let the weight go.

Changing Habits

Letting go of the emotional reasons for holding the weight is an enormous step forward, but anyone wishing to lose weight will have given consideration to adjusting some of the physical and life-style habits they have adopted over the years that have supported them in using weight as protection.

I would definitely recommend to anyone that has a weight issue that they feel to be impacted by experiences and traumas like sexual attack, that they do the *Radical Empowerment* Program. Using it over a period of six to 12 months will not only help to complete all the *Radical Forgiveness* that might need to be done, but will help in making the other life-style changes as well.

---

*A morphogenetic field and morphic resonance are terms coined by biologist, Rupert Sheldrake, author of *A New Science of Life,* 1995, to explain how information is transferred energetically between people irrespective of distance.

PART SIX

Purpose

Chapter 21
Finding Your Purpose

In order to give direction and focus to any decision, you would think that defining the purpose for it should come first, and that by placing this chapter at the end of the book I have, so to speak, put the cart before the horse. I believe it does belong here, though, because with this kind of book the end IS the beginning. It's where we start putting it all into practice — or not. Assuming that we do, there is no better question to ask yourself before going into action than "What is my purpose?"

By asking this question, I am requiring of myself that I give meaning and focus to my life. Also, in the context of this book, it helps in deciding what I want to manifest.

Herein lies another good reason for posing the question late in the book, for the answers you will give will depend on your cosmology.

If you believe in the old paradigm as described in Chapter Four, where life is purely a game of chance with little or no meaning to it, the purpose you will see for your own life within that system will likely be quite different from how you will see it if you perceive the world from the metaphysical viewpoint. I am going to assume, therefore, that having got this far in the book, you are at least willing to allow me to frame the discussion about purpose in the context of the latter paradigm rather that the former.

The Overall Purpose for Being Human
In several places in the book I have alluded to there being an overall purpose for us being here. As I see it — and it is only something I make up — the grand purpose of our existence in physical form is to expand the Mind of God.

In order to explain this idea, let me be self-indulgent and give you an excerpt from my own book, *A Radical Incarnation.** This is a story in which a soul named Jack is being prepared for its upcoming incarnation by Harley, his Angel of Incarnation. The following is part of a conversation between the two of them about this idea of God (Universal Intelligence) expanding its consciousness.

. . . . Harley picked up exactly where he had left off.

"Earlier in our discourse I sidetracked the issue of all this being purposeful in terms of the need that Universal Intelligence has to continue expanding its consciousness. Let's deal with it now because it is central to everything.

---

*See Appendix, Page 207

"Jack, do you have any idea how Universal Intelligence and everything else came into being?"

"Not really," I said, looking at all the others to make sure I was not the only one in ignorance of something so vitally important. "But I would like to know. I've never questioned it before. I have always taken it for granted that Universal Intelligence had always existed."

"Well, not exactly," said Harley. "Let me try to explain it to you as simply as I can. It is not easy to comprehend, so pay attention.

"You've heard of the Big Bang theory, haven't you? Humans have spent a long time developing this theory and to tell you the truth, they are not far off the mark. The only bit they haven't yet fully understood is of course the most important part of the whole thing. And that is the bit about what was prior to the Big Bang. Because they are so locked into the idea of time and space, they can't imagine anything coming into being without there being something before. It's a real problem for them.

"The truth is though that there was nothing before the Big Bang. Except consciousness – pure potential that's all. That is until consciousness gave birth to the very first thought."

"What was that?" I asked nervously.

"What if there is something else?" Harley replied dramatically.

"That's it?"

"That was it," said Harley. "In the very instant that this thought occurred within that field of consciousness, the Big Bang occurred. The material universe manifested immediately in that very moment and in that instant Universal Consciousness became intelligent. God was."

Harley stood there looking triumphant as if he himself had been solely responsible for the Big Bang. We all stood there speechless, but he was so excited he hardly drew breath before going on.

"As you know from your previous studies, the material universe has continued to grow and expand. Scientists have actually measured the rate at which it is expanding. However, just as the material universe has continued to grow and expand, so has Universal Intelligence. God needs to continue expanding its consciousness in exactly the same way, for it too is part of that same expanding universe. You will notice that even on earth people talk about God as 'the Universe.' This is no accident.

"Anyway, having unleashed the potential for infinite creativity Universal Intelligence created us and all other intelligent life forms so it could continue its expansion. Indeed that is the only reason Universal Intelligence created us."

"How so?" we asked, more or less in unison.

"Since Universal Intelligence could not experience itself as itself, it created us so that it could continue to experience itself through us in ever expanding ways, in tune with the expanding universe. That is what is meant when we say that God is our Father and we are the son of God.

174

"Now, here's where it gets interesting," said Harley, leaning over to get closer to us as if he was about to share something of great value. "Without us, God isn't."

"I don't get it. What are you saying, Harley?" I said.

"Look, Jack, I think you are trying to make it too difficult," said Harley, somewhat impatiently. "It's really quite simple. God created us and gave us the ability to go in and out of that world of duality and physicality....."

"You mean the world of form that arose out of that first thought and the subsequent Big Bang?" I interrupted.

"Exactly," said Harley, continuing. "..... so it could experience that world vicariously through us. That way Universal Intelligence would continue to expand in tune with the physical universe.

"We are vital to that expansion, Jack. Each and every soul who incarnates and all of those who, like your team here, support that process, is playing a vital role in expanding God's consciousness. That's what I mean when I say that without us, God isn't. Without you, Jack, God isn't."

"So, once I take on a human body, I am God in physical form playing in the physical realm. Is that right?"

"Yes," Harley confirmed. "It is as if the hand of God has put on a glove – and you are that glove. Without that glove Universal Intelligence could not experience the physical world. Are you clear now why you are doing it and what it's all about?"

"Well, clearer than I was, that's for sure," I responded. "I certainly hadn't any notion of how my journey would be about being in service to the whole idea of Universal Intelligence expanding its consciousness. Up to then I had thought it was more about me as a spiritual being, growing in awareness of what Universal Intelligence — or God — really is."

"That is true too," replied Harley. "But let's talk about that after the break."

And then later on in the book Harley further explains:

"The basic aim of taking this human journey is to experience the opposite of what we know to be the truth up here – ONE-NESS and LOVE. Through the experience of those opposites we can come to know ONENESS and LOVE more fully and through that awareness move to a whole new level in our spiritual growth and expand even more the consciousness of Universal Intelligence. With me up to now, Jack?"

"Sure."

"You also will recall that the human experience will set you up to be abandoned, rejected, betrayed, terrorized, and perhaps even tortured during your earth walk. Those are just some examples of things that will help you fully experience the opposites of LOVE and ONENESS. OK, Jack?"

"Well, I guess it's OK. Can't say I'm looking forward to all that though."

"Hey, don't imagine that life is only that," Harley warned. "A great deal of the human experience is totally wonderful and marvellous. In fact I would venture to say that the majority of

*it is this way. There are many wonderful opportunities to ex-
perience LOVE and bliss, harmony and peace every day.*

*"We shall see later, these high vibration experiences are just
as important to our spiritual growth as the seemingly less pleas-
ant experiences. In fact, there may come a time when, having
transcended and given up the victim archetype, we will derive
the greatest spiritual growth not from adversity and pain but
from the experience of beauty, compassion, gratitude and other
wonderful things that feed the spirit.*

*"However, at this time all humans are, by their own choice,
still addicted to victimhood, pain and suffering so it's to there
that the energy naturally flows. Since it is a principle that spiritual growth occurs wherever the energy is most in motion, humans will still tend to use these as their catalysts for growth
rather than the more positive experiences. Maybe that will
change soon and they will be able to choose experiences based
in joy and harmony as their catalyst for growth.*

*"Of course, whether it changes or not is inconsequential to us
in this world, Jack. We up here, you see, are not attached to
what kind of experiences they use to create growth. Our only
concern is that growth occurs and that it leads to a clear remembrance of who we are and expands the consciousness of
ONENESS.*

*"Their current focus on the seemingly negative experiences
just reflects the prevailing human appetite for the energy attached to pain and suffering — and especially that associated
with victimhood. Wherever the energy is, we follow. That's
how it is!"*

177

Tongue-in-Cheek

And so the conversation continues for about two-thirds of the book. Of course, it is tongue-in-cheek, but it nevertheless accords with the idea, central to *Radical Forgiveness,* that everything is happening for a reason, that there is meaning and PURPOSE in everything that happens.

Such a story serves a purpose in helping us connect with the feelings that tell us we are connected to Universal Intelligence (God) and that Universal Intelligence dwells within each of us. It is also gives us a powerful way to frame our purpose for being on this planet according to our own individual creation story.

Individual Purpose

That said, now let's focus our attention on our individual purpose. Gaining clarity about our purpose is no different than gaining clarity about other aspects of our lives. Just as we discovered that getting clarity about what we want to manifest is a matter of how we feel about it, the same is true of our purpose. When we become infused with good feelings, like inspiration, passion and joy, we know that we have found our purpose.

Connecting with our purpose helps us to focus our energy in such a way as to transcend our limited definitions of who we are and become empowered to be all that we can be. It enables us to focus on what we might want to manifest in our lives that will, in turn, give meaning to, and support us in, aligning with our purpose.

Levels of Purpose

But in the same way that we created three levels of intentions, with the lowest refering to the one above, it seems to me that we need to do the same for purpose. My purpose for having agreed to this human journey might, therefore, be expressed hierachically as follows:

Level One: To expand the Mind of God.

Level Two: To experience duality and separation as a way of expanding our consciousness of Oneness and Love.

Level Three: To express, in the best way I can, with all that I have been given, the essence of my own humanity.

The first two are way beyond our comprehension and conscious awareness and occur at the level of soul agreement. How we experience the separation, to what extent, and with whom we create it, is determined by our soul and those souls who guide us, and manifests in the world of form through our spiritual intelligence. In that sense our purpose is given to us. If, at in any particular moment in time our Divine purpose is to be a murderer, there is nothing we can do about it. At this level, it is not our game.

The third level is the only level at which we get to play. It is the only level where we consciously and unconsciously use our own knowledge, awareness, values, understanding, motivations, talents and skills to express our purpose.

179

And everyone plays. No one is excluded and to the extent that this purpose references the purposes at levels one and two, no one is doing it any better or worse than anyone else. That means no one person's purpose is better or worse than anyone else's, any more than anyone is further along in their spiritual path than anyone else. In my view there is no such thing as a spiritual elite. We are all on a spiritual path and we are all where we need to be.

However, wherever we are on our journey will determine whether we are able to reference our purpose to the two levels above or not. If we are still in Victimland, our purpose is likely to be expressed in low level, materialistic and survivalist terms, and that's OK. Only when, at some pre-planned moment, we begin to wake up to the truth and emerge from Victimland, will we be able to see our purpose in terms of the bigger picture and align with the two higher level purposes. And that's perfect too.

To support the discussion about purpose from here on, I am going to assume that you have arrived at this point. I doubt that you would be reading this book if you were not.

As I said earlier, formulating our purpose gives our life meaning, clarity and focus. Framing it in terms of Level One and Two helps us give a larger context to our purpose, but after that it is a matter of coming down to earth to discover it within ourselves.

Here is a method of discovering your purpose which I have found to be simple and effective.

Process For Discovering Your Purpose

1. Make a list of all your talents, skills, capabilities, interests and personal qualities that you are aware of.

Example:
>*Creative*
>*Artistic (painter)*
>*Patient*
>*Good researcher*
>*Good with people*
>*Good with children*
>*Good speaker*
>*Musicianship*
>*Academic*
>*Dance*

2. Ask some people close to you — friends, family, colleagues, etc., what skills, talents, qualities and capabilities they see in you and appreciate about you. Make a separate list of these, even if some of them are duplicates. Make a note of those that you did not recognize in yourself.

Example:
>*Musical talent Good leader* Friendly**
>*Compassionate* Teaching Ability**

* Did not list myself.

181

3. Rate each one on a scale of 0-100 according to the level of proficiency you have in each of the skills and talents on the list. Zero is none whatsoever, while 100 would be total mastery. 50 would be average proficiency. Be as objective as you can about this. Ask others if necessary.

Example:

Creative	*70*
Artistic (painter)	*40*
Patient	
Good researcher	*40*
Good with people	
Good with children	
Good speaker	*30*
Musicianship	*60*
Academic	*40*
Dance	*20*
Good leader	*50*
Friendly	
Compassionate	
Teaching Ability	*60*

4. Rate each one on a scale of 0-100 according to how much **passion** you have for expressing each one of the items on the lists. Zero would mean you hate doing it and would never do it by choice. 100 would mean that it gives you total joy and you resent every moment that you are not doing it. 50 would mean you don't feel strongly either way. In other words you quite enjoy doing it when you are, but wouldn't necessarily go out of your way to do it. Be careful not to score them on the basis of how much approval it gets you. That might feel good but it is secondary to the feeling that arises simply out of doing it. One way to check this is to note how you feel in your gut when you say the word or think about expressing that quality or talent. Is it positive or negative? Does is make you feel good, or not?

Example:

	Proficiency	*Passion*
Creative	*70*	*80*
Artistic (painter)	*40*	*95*
Patience		*60*
Good researcher	*40*	*5*
Good with people		*20*
Good with children		*60*
Good speaker	*30*	*10*
Musicianship	*60*	*70*
Academic	*40*	*10*
Dance	*20*	*40*
Good leader	*20*	*20*
Friendly		*50*
Compassion		*60*
Teaching Ability	*60*	*70*

Note: Proficiency does not necessarily equate with passion or even enjoyment. This person is good academically and good at research, but enjoys neither. His/her painting skill is the same as those two and not great, but he or she shows enormous passion for the activity.

5. Select up to five items that score high on the passion scale, irrespective of how much proficiency you have in each one, and then write down how you like to express them.

Example:
> *Creativity*
> *Artistic (painter)*
> *Musicianship*
> *Teaching Ability*

Creativity:
I like to express my creativity by exploring new ways of seeing things and expressing my perceptions visually through painting in all sorts of different media, dance and music.

Painting:
I love to lose myself in the painting process and in expressing my feelings that way, learn about myself and the world around me because I see everything in new and exciting ways.

Musicianship:
I love to play the piano and keyboard instruments and to experiment with sounds and harmonies that I can relate to my painting in a mult-media format.

Teaching Ability:
I love working with children because they are so creative and free when allowed to be so. I seem to be able to bring that out in them.

6. Create a grandiose purpose statement of what you would be achieving or doing if you were expressing all these talents in the way that would be totally enjoyable to you and where there are no limits on you.

Example:

"My purpose is to use my compassion, my patience, and my ability to inspire children in awakening and nurturing their creative spirit through expressing my passion for artistic endeavour through painting, dance and music as a demonstration to them of the power of the arts to bring joy to millions of people."

7. Now edit it down to a short memorable statement. The above statement covers all the bases, but it is long and cumbersome. It would be hard to remember. A purpose statement needs to be something you repeat often, so it should be short, easy to say and easily memorized.

Example:

My purpose is to inspire all children to free their creative spirit and to find joy in the creative process, while I too soar in my own creative power as an artist.

8. Check to see if you have it right, by registering how it feels to you. Keep massaging it until it feels good, like it really fits. If it doesn't feel wonderful, look again to see it you have put the wrong thing first. For instance, in this example, the lists show that the real juice was in being the

185

artist, especially painting which he or she scored at (95). Children and teaching came in at (60 and (70) respectively. I would want to ask whether this person was actually selling out by going for what seemed possible or achievable rather than what was really in his or her heart?

Let's try it again. Here's another version of *#7* where the painting becomes the primary purpose and the teaching of children secondary:

"My purpose is to change the way that millions of people see the world by using my skill as a painter, musician and dancer to bring them to a new understanding of reality and employ my teaching ability to open the hearts and minds of children to the joy in the creative process."

And then, edited down:

"My purpose is to change the world through my art by opening people's eyes to what is meaningful while freeing the creative spirit in children."

This seems more in alignment with his or her real purpose. It doesn't matter that the proficiency is not yet very high. That can be attained through training. Getting the training is exactly the thing this person can use the *Radical Manifestation* technology to create. With that much intention (95 percent passion), it is virtually guaranteed!

Afterword
By JoAnn Tipping

W hen I read the draft of this book, I said to my husband, "Where's the chapter on gratitude? Isn't that a big part of the manifestation process — feeling gratitude for what you want, in advance?"

"I've made reference to it a lot, but it doesn't have its own chapter," he replied. "Would you like to write an afterword on gratitude, to really make the point?" Well, I could hardly refuse, could I?

I think of gratitude as that wonderful feeling of thankfulness and appreciation we feel when we see that we are blessed with something. It's a great feeling. But feeling it in advance? That's not so easy. How do you make yourself feel it when what you are trying to feel thankful for is not there yet?

The answer is practice. It's a skill like all the other things that Colin talks about in Chapter 13. I learned this myself one dark and rainy evening when I was driving home from a *Course in Miracles* class. I had arrived there feeling depressed and tired, and I had left feeling much the same.

We had worked on Lesson # 344 in the Workbook: *"Today I learn the law of love; that what I give my brother is my gift to me. . . . Let my forgiven brothers fill my store with Heaven's treasures, which alone are real."* We talked about giving and receiving being the same and how gratitude could arise out of either. Even though I was still in a funk, I decided that on the way home I would try to look for the "Heaven's treasures" in my own life.

I felt a lot of resistance to doing it and it seemed impossible at first. I really wanted to focus on what was not good in my life as a way to feed my negative feelings. But I just started with what was there in front of me.

I am grateful for the rain.
I am grateful for the night time.
I am grateful for the car that is getting me home safely.
I am grateful for the headlights that show me the way.
I am grateful for my own eyes through which I see.
. . . and so on.

I began to recognize that I had so much of Heaven's treasure that I was incredibly abundant and the feeling of gratitude began to sweep over me. I had started out very much in present time, but I found myself going back in time to things that I was thankful for in my childhood. Tears came spontaneously as I realized all the little things that, at the time, I had been very upset about but could now feel thankful for. One thing in particular came up that I had always considered to be a disaster in my life. I had flunked second grade because I had hepatitis and was out of school for four months in quarantine. But now I saw the perfection in that situation as well and felt the gratitude.

Speaking all these things out loud as I wound down the road at 9:15 in the evening, toasty warm in my car, I was crying and laughing as the words of gratitude came falling out of my mouth, one sentence after another. I allowed no thought to get in the way of whatever came as a thank you or a homage to gratitude for my teachers, lovers, pets, traffic lights or bumps in the road. It was an exhilarating experience that filled me with joy and insights that may never have come out in any other way. It was an 'out-loud allowing' of love and gratitude that lasted a full 30 minutes.

When I got home I was in a state of pure bliss and joy. My tiredness and depression had disappeared completely. Simply through making expressions of gratitude, in spite of not wanting to at the outset, I had transformed myself.

Had I known about *Radical Manifestation* at that time I probably would have reached for a *Radical Manifestation* worksheet and asked for all that I wanted right there and then, for I believe I had enough gratitude in my soul at that moment to have attracted almost anything.

What I did, though, was pull out a piece of calligraphy that was entitled Abundance. The original text was by Arnold M. Patent, given at a workshop in September 1991. The workshop was entitled Celebration of Abundance and I was there. I would like to share this with you. I think it is a good way to end this book because it expresses the very essence of the message it contains. Read it often.

Blessings,
JoAnn.

Abundance

Abundance is the natural state of affairs
in the Universe.

I release all resistance to abundance.
I feel the release of all resistance to abundance.
I open myself to receive abundance.
I feel myself sharing abundance generously with others.
As I give and receive love, I feel myself
opening to abundance.
My willingness to receive lovingly from others is my
way of supporting other in giving to themselves.

My willingness to give lovingly to others is my way
of giving to myself.
I now feel abundance flowing to others and back to me.
I now feel abundance flowing to the Universe and
back to me.
I now feel gratitude for the gift I have just given
and received

I know and feel that abundance in the natural state of
the affairs in the Universe and I give thanks for it.

Arnold M. Patent

190

APPENDIX

APPENDIX

Colin Tipping's
Radical Empowerment Program

Imagine being able to create the life you want! This program empowers you to make that happen.

Package Contents

DVD - Empowerment Through Radical Forgiveness
DVD - The Soul's Journey - The Metaphysics of RF/RE
DVD - The Tools of *Radical Forgiveness*
DVD - Radical Relationships
DVD - *Radical Self-Forgiveness & Self-Acceptance*
CD - 13 Steps to *Radical Forgiveness*
CD - 13 Steps to *Radical Self-Forgiveness*
CD - 13 Steps to *Radical Manifestation*
CD - The *Radical Forgiveness* Meditations
CD - Spiritual Intelligence Training Processes
Printed Pad of *Radical Forgiveness* Worksheets
Printed Pad of *Radical Self-Forgiveness* Worksheets
Printed Pad of *Radical Manifestation* Worksheets
Printed *Radical Empowerment* "Miracles" Journal
Book *"Radical Manifestation"* by Colin Tipping

How It Works —It gives you the tools that activate the power within you to create virtually anything you desire.It teaches you how to use your *spiritual intelligence* to raise your vibration, create your reality and accelerate your spiritual growth.

A Powerful Technology —The combination of *Radical Forgiveness* (to heal the past) and *Radical Empowerment* (to create the future), is a very simple technology, but the effects are dramatic. The struggle is over. You simply take the information provided and put it into practice, using the Spiritual Intelligence Training Processes to *supercharge the results.*

A 12-Month Program

We recommend that for optimum effect, you commit to working this program for about 12 months. By the end of that period, your vibration should be significantly higher and your ability to manifest your reality will be much enhanced.

For the High Flyers - The "500 Club" Program

For those who wish to take this to the next level, and are willing to make a deeper commitment to their spiritual growth, either during or subsequent to doing this program, they can join our "500 Club" program. The objective is to reach and operate consistently at a vibration of around 500 on the Hawkins Scale of Consciousness — the point at which you shift into a different level of awareness and begin changing the world.

Details at *www.radicalempowerment.com*

No Risk, Money-Back Guarantee

If, after you have received and reviewed the program you are not happy with it, you may return it in good condition within a period of 30 days and receive all your money back, no questions asked.

The Radical Empowerment Tools

Worksheets:
Radical Manifestation Worksheet*
Money Consciousness Worksheet*
Radical Forgiveness Worksheet
Radical Self-Forgiveness Worksheet
4 Steps to Radical Forgiveness Worksheet
The Centrifuge Worksheet
The Grief Assessment Worksheet*
The Release Letter

On-line Tools
The Radical Forgiveness Worksheet Tutorial (FREE)
Radical Self-Forgiveness On-line Program
Radical Self-Acceptance On-line Program
Releasing Secrets On-line Program

Processes:
13 Steps to Radical Forgiveness (Audio)
13 Steps to Radical SELF Forgiveness (Audio)
The Three Letters Forgiveness Process (Written)
The 4-Step Empowerment Process (Internal Process)
CD: Radical Forgiveness Meditations
CD: 13 Steps to Radical Manifestation Process*
CD: Spiritual Intelligence Training Processes*
    i. Morning Intentional Meditation (2 mins.)
    ii Evening Gratitude Meditation (2 mins.)
    iii Supercharging Your Intentions (Short Audio)
    iv Supercharging Your Intentions (Long Audio)

Processes Facilitated by Certified Radical Forgiveness and Radical Empowerment Coaches
RF & RE Coaching (in person or by phone)
The 'Satori' 7-Step Process to Radical Forgiveness
Etheric Cleansing Process

* These items available only in the *Radical Empowerment* Program.

Radical Empowerment Workshops and Certification Training Programs

1. Workshops
We regularly offer a variety of ways of experiencing Radical Forgiveness and Radical Empowerment in a group setting, so take a look at our web site, *www.radicalforgiveness.com* for descriptions of the workshops and check the schedule for dates.

2. Online Programs
A FREE, interactive *Radical Forgiveness* process is available on our web site for anyone to use at any time. We also offer three on-line programs for SELF-EMPOWERMENT. These are self-guided and can be done at your own pace.
      a) Radical Self-Forgiveness Program
      b) Radical Self-Acceptance Program
      c) Releasing Toxic Secrets Program

Go to ***www.onlinehealingprograms.com*** for details

3. Certification Training Programs
If you like to teach, run book study groups, coach others and to be of service to people, or you are already in the healing arts or mental health professions, you might wish to examine our training programs. They offer certification as:

a) Certified Book Study Leader

b) Certified Radical Empowerment Discussion Group Leader

c) Certified Teacher of Radical Forgiveness

d) Certified Radical Forgiveness Coach

e) Certified Coach/RF Ceremony Facilitator

f) Certified Radical Forgiveness Therapy Practitioner
                      (This is for already qualified mental health practitioners)

For details go to www.radicalforgiveness.com

"I LOVE This Book!"

says **Caroline Myss,** Ph.D.
author of 'Sacred Contracts'

"The most exciting book on forgiveness to come out in a very long time. I have never seen anything so well written and so 'right on the money,' on this topic."

Neale Donald Walsch
author of 'Conversations With God'

Radical Forgiveness:
Making Room for the Miracle
By Colin Tipping

This is the book that started it all. Released in 1997, it won a Writer's Digest Award in 1998 and it has continued to change the lives of people all around the world ever since.

The technology of *Radical Forgiveness* forms the basis of the *Radical Empowerment* technology so is highly recommended as a companion book to this book.

Colin Tipping is dedicated to bringing **RADICAL Forgiveness** to the world in a form that is easy to understand, easy to accomplish, easy to integrate into a lifestyle and above all, practical. He has achieved that in this one very important book!

Available in bookstores or *www.radicalforgiveness.com*

197

'Satori'

The Radical Forgiveness Game

The *Radical Forgiveness* experience can be had in many different ways. This board game is the most recent, and is now available.

As you would expect, it takes you through the same five stages of *Radical Forgiveness,* but this time in the context of a game that can be played by up to five people and takes between 1-1/2 and 2-1/2 hours to play.

It is a lot of fun, and in the playing of it, energy is moved in the same mysterious way as it does in all the other forms of the *Radical Forgiveness* Experience.

It is not neccesary for all players have prior knowledge of *Radical Forgiveness.*

Players pick a 'story' card to play with *(which invariably resonates a real situation for them)*, and they all start in Victimland. They proceed around the board which spirals in towards the center, the objective being to reach the full Satori, which is, as you know, the Awakening. We find ourselves picking up beliefs and energy blocks along the way, finding ways to release them, or project them onto someone else. There are three Gateways to get through — the Gateway to Awareness; the Gateway to Shift Happens and the Gateway to Surrender.

There are no winners or losers. The game ends when everyone reaches Satori and joyfully reads out their reframe.

This game is available now!
Check it out on the web site —
you'll love it! Invite your friends!
Great gift idea!

Spirituality in Business is HOT —

This __Book__ is Hot!

A <u>MUST-READ</u> for anyone interested in being at the forefront of
the new business cultural revolu-
tion characterized as *'social capi-
talism.'* It shows how a cutting-
edge, employee development system that uses a spiritual viewpoint,
the **Quantum Energy Management System,*** can transform the
culture of any organization in ways
that benefit everyone involved —
while boosting the bottom line.

<u>**An audio CD is included as a sample of the technology.**</u>

In this ground-breaking book, Colin Tipping shows how any
organization can be transformed with this enterprise-wide, personal development program that:

- *reduces* incidents of conflict, discord, dissent,
  sabotage, cynicism, racial tension, etc.

- *Increases* morale, job satisfaction, loyalty,
  cooperation, team spirit and overall productivity.

**A Radical Approach to Increasing Productivity, Raising
Morale and Preventing Conflict in the Workplace.**

Global 13 Publications, Inc.
Hardbound with Dust Cover; 240 Pages; USA $23.95

* For information about **The Quantum Energy Management
System** go to www.QEMSystem.com

A Radical Incarnation

*"The President of the United States Becomes Enlightened, Heals America and Awakens Humanity - **A Spiritual Fantasy"***

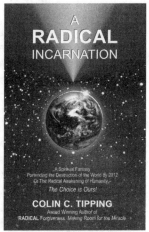

Colin Tipping has a real gift for making spiritual principles simple and applicable to everyday life.

He has done it again with this book, bringing that ability to bear on the much larger issues of the day – principally **world peace.**

The way he does it is that you, the reader, gets to accompany the soul of Jack Barber as he is carefully tutored and prepared by Harley, his senior Angel of Incarnation, for his upcoming human experience on planet Earth, along with another soul with whom he will interact on the world stage to bring the world to a point of breakdown and then break*through.* Could it be . . . ?

Is it possible that these two souls made a soul agreement to do this? Is Saddam a *"healing angel"* for America, mirroring its shadow? Are we playing a part too? ***You bet we are!***

Colin's mission is ***"to raise the consciousness of the planet through Radical Forgiveness and to create a world of forgiveness by 2012."*** His unstated agenda for creating the

Radical Empowerment Program is to empower enough people to make this happen. He cannot do it alone.

It will have occurred to you by now that the power you have to create your own reality includes the possibility of creating a wholly different world. A radically empowered person can literally create world peace. And it only takes a few of us to actually form the critical mass necessary to make it happen.

We can't look to this or any other president to awaken and lead humanity to do the same. We must do it. It is not Jack Barber's or even George Bush's "radical incarnation." It's yours. It's ours.

As with his other books, Colin provides the on-line technology with which to transform ourselves and — hopefully without the need for breakdown — to heal America, raise the consciousness of the planet and create Heaven on Earth.

Go to *www.radicalforgiveness.com* and click on the **America's Healing Project** link on the Home page. You will get an invitation to participate in the process of creating world peace by:

1. Forgiving America's enemies, including Saddam, bin Laden and others
2. Forgiving America and its leaders
3. Forgiving yourself and your personal enemies
4. Making a Radical Apology to blacks, Native Americans, Jews etc.
5. Accepting a Radical Apology, if due
6. Empower a vision of world peace

The Secret to the Creation of World Peace is Radical Empowerment!